LETTING GO
OF THE THIEF

"A NINETY DAY JOURNEY INSIDE THE THOUGHTS OF AN ALCOHOLIC."

PAMELA D. PESTA

outskirts
press

To my sons... Nicholas and William,
The thief comes to kill and destroy. I chose to
have life abundantly. Where there is darkness,
light can always prevail. I stand in it now,
because I love you both with all my heart.

Table of Contents

Dear Reader,

My desire in writing this book is that you may be transported into real alcoholic thinking. This is a harrowing disease which effects not only the problem drinker, but those who love him/her. Unfortunately, everyone gets dragged through the mud until that choice for recovery is finally made.

Alcoholics Anonymous is a gift of hope for everyone. Most sponsors will tell their alcoholic sponsee to attend ninety meetings in ninety days. This discipline opens the door to sober friendships, empathetic understanding, and spiritual growth in recovery. Thus, I wrote this journey using this ninety-day thought process, conveying the absolute struggles and the incredible triumphs.

The deliberations described within these pages are an accounting of other alcoholics, as well as my own. Our stories may be different, but our outcomes much the same. The bottle ran our lives with a furious contempt. We were ultimately left living in a world filled with shame.

I hovered once in those shadows until I finally surrendered and accepted that I had a problem. I am free now, living a beautiful life in the arms of serenity. My quest is that you might let go of the thief and walk toward the light of sobriety, where you will discover that person you were truly meant to be.

The Thief...

I couldn't find you, even when you were standing directly in front of me. I couldn't hear you, even when you began shouting. I couldn't embrace you, even when you tried to pull me forward. I couldn't console you, even as tears fell down your face. I couldn't accept your desire to help me, even though I understood that if I didn't, I might truly lose you.

By the time I came to realize this, the poison of alcohol was already pulsating through my bloodstream like a thief in the night. And it was there, where my soul chose the silent darkness of the bottle. The choice to choose you was no longer mine to make. The thief assured me that I would taste an amazing freedom once you were gone. A lifetime guarantee of painless days, where coping with the world would be effortless.

Swiftly and yet slowly, I opted for his cunning promises. Each passing drink granted me the ability to dismiss those edgy reminders of how I never felt like part of the crowd. I became empowered to move forward gracefully in life, without the nagging undertones of constant discouragement and fear. Alcohol converted my real feelings of inadequacy into strength and fortitude. It gave me permission to enter into the foggy realm of forgetting. This snare of unconscious living tendered the perfect escape.

At first, I made a few silly mistakes when drinking a bit too much, but nobody seemed to notice. The thief and I were becoming fast friends, so he kindly offered some helpful hints on how to behave. It all seemed easy enough, and I was usually satisfied with the results. But, there were days when my soul recognized that something horribly powerful was gnawing at my very core, and I knew right down to the bone that it was him. Even so, his hushed prodding overpowered any fleeting sense of my uncertainty.

It went on like that for quite some time...for years really. Eventually, it became clear that I needed more alcohol to achieve instant relief. My mistakes while drinking were becoming more apparent to me, and I couldn't face that reality. The thief smirked in the shadowy corner with an immediate suggestion; he was eager to please. "Forget wine and beer; liquor is much more soothing, and nobody will know."

I grappled with this idea, quickly resolving that I ought to give it a try. I liked the effects of this change almost immediately. It was working so well, that I began allowing myself a few drinks in the afternoon. I loved the sensation of imaginary tranquility during my daylight hours. Miraculously, my innermost worries were easily resolved and shelved away until tomorrow. I embraced this sly, mysterious reprieve with gratitude.

It was a beautiful epiphany for a while...until I noticed some slipups. My secret world was being interfered with. People were noticing what I was doing, and they were trying to trap me. Their superior ridicule consumed my thoughts. I didn't like how my sacred routine was suddenly being questioned. But it was also becoming obvious that my purposely hidden fears were dissolving into hatred, anger, and total chaos for everyone else.

I clearly knew that something had to be done to regain some sensibility. I knew that I was somehow hurting you deeply by my daily actions. So I tried, when I could, to stop drinking. And if that didn't work, I aimed at other solutions: keep to beer, soundly monitor myself at parties, try to keep my mouth shut when I was having a few too many, be less challenging, and above all…always look like a normal drinker.

For a short time, I was able to maintain this strategy. I tried hard to ignore the thief's cutting reminders of a better way out, until finally, my hopeful resistance to his tirades fell apart. It became painfully apparent to me that I needed the drink. My pointless attempts at trying to stop only made me restless and aching for that safer place where I could dissolve my anxiety and growing pain. Of course, I irrationally convinced myself that this decision would be best for both of us.

Without pause, I glided into the arms of a hopeful oblivion, where I could love you, and accept my personal challenges equally, as long as the thief could come too. I was totally in control of this titanic effort, this momentous resolution which would surely benefit our future.

In no time at all, my virtuous goals and well-meaning efforts began to wane. The more I followed the thief, the more destruction I caused. The more gulps of liquor I took, the more steps I took to hide from you. This insidious progression tormented me, and I realized that I could no longer tolerate who I had become at your expense.

I eagerly searched for a different solution, but the only one that came was the drink. For it was with it that I could remove myself from the heartache I was causing you, and, better yet, forget. I began to go away then. I don't think it was a conscious decision; I had simply run out of options. I had come to believe that I could no longer adapt to your world without the thief. You didn't want this. You made polite requests; you made loud ones. You pushed and pulled; you cried out for me. I placidly watched you grieve for who I had become, but I could not alter my desperation for the bottle. My broken spirit, so filled with utter remorse and absolute shame, could no longer embrace your undying love for me.

With a hopelessness not meant for words, I turned toward the thief in some meaningless acceptance of my fate. I was weary and tired. I had let you go. I had made my choice to walk toward madness and probable death. Grimmer still, I could not stop myself for the sake of you, not even for the sake of you.

There, in the lonely solitude of terror, I began my daily ritual. Bottle after bottle, after emptied bottle. There, in that battlefield of desperation and total despair, I slowly disappeared into a lifeless entity of emptiness. If I saw you I no longer recognized you, nor were you able to recognize me. I had grown numb to the core, which allowed me to dismiss even the slightest sense of you. By then, I was already strolling in the graveyard, plotting my eventual end.

My fears grew as I watched myself spiral downward. I knew that the thief had stolen everything from me. Each morning I bartered and pleaded with God to give me the strength to start over again. But somehow, that almighty bottle made its way into my hands with increasing misery and brutal anguish. My mental state was fading, and my physical body was being beaten. I began to accept the shaking and vomiting as normal.

My shoddy appearance grew comfortable—passing out, falling into fitful nightmares, a welcome.

Every value, every principle, every sane thought had been diminished. The mundane darkness swirled around me with contemptuous might. My soul ached with the thought of you, as my body dragged on in some bleak crawl space of inhumanity. I was worn to the very core.

I can't recall how I saw you there, standing in the shadows between my world and yours. I could barely open my eyes, but I noticed. For a moment, I felt a warmth, a stirring of timeless recognition. My heart beat to the old memory of you, and I sighed with a breath of relief. But before I could nod toward your kind face, the thief came running toward me. Confusion set in, panic overwhelmed me, and you faded away.

Soon thereafter, I saw you again, and then again. Gradually, I began to hear you; I knew that your soft voice was not imagined. In hushed, kindhearted tones, you begged me to return. Suddenly, a shimmering light flowed from your corner, and your image grew clearer. Your presence began to permeate the perimeter of my bleak dungeon, illuminating the heavy chains binding me there. I hadn't noticed them before. My eyes widened as I seriously started to observe my dismal surroundings.

As more light streamed toward me, I was taken aback by the pounding revelation of my whereabouts. My anguished screams echoed from the cold cement walls with humiliating intensity. I looked down at the shattered remains of emptied bottles scattered beneath my feet. I could feel my clothing clinging to my skin, reeking of destitution and sweat. The rotting odor of emptiness permeated my senses.

My body began fitfully trembling as I came to recognize

that the thief had been lying to me all along. I was merely his prisoner, who had become enslaved by his fruitless promises. I looked at you in disbelief and profound horror. I was broken and terribly afraid. My mind whirled with fearful questions and hopeful possibilities that I might risk it all and run from the thief. His version of living hadn't been living at all. The proof was staring at me from the gray depths of that long-ago choice which had confined me to this miserable place.

I suddenly understood that I could no longer live like this. A desperate, unfulfilled life was glaring directly at me. Something had always been missing, and I could feel the urgency of this loss. I frantically needed the light; I knew that I must rush toward it before the thief could recognize that I was gone. I nervously began to stand, lifting my chin toward you, as tears of relief flowed down my face. I bravely placed my hand in yours, feeling the warmth of hopeful expectation and optimistic release as you pulled me toward freedom. For the first time in years, I finally felt safe.

You had always been there, of course. You had been there from the beginning, watching, waiting, and mercifully trying to protect me from my inevitable ruin. You had always prayed, and you had always held on. And even in the darkest hours, I had always known that I needed to return, because deep within the crevices of my heart, I had always loved you too.

I Am Powerless
Over Alcohol

I am powerless over alcohol. One drink will lead me to another. One glistening bottle or tiny glassful will have my mind whirling for more. I will not cease in my need to keep swallowing. I will not stop because you have asked me to. My desire will increase with each passing hour. My aspirations will change. Your welfare and dignity will no longer be my concern. I will impulsively turn away, leaving you to rot with unmanageable expectations. You will suddenly grasp that I have become a stranger.

I am powerless over alcohol. An innocent sip of it will take me to a world which you will never fully understand. I will perplex you with my obsessive desire for it. My yearning will overpower your grief for me. I will not see you as I once did. My mental state will become aggravated and crazed. I will openly follow my ultimate need to sustain my intake. The force of my resolve will not allow you to enter this place. The bottle will replace you.

I am powerless over alcohol. A mere taste of this pulsating liquid will harm both of us. The force of this intoxication will increase with every gulp. You will quickly be set aside because of it. You will not be able to reach me. I, in turn, will be glad that you can't. I will not see any immediate consequences. I will grant myself unconscious reprieve from the likes of tomorrow.

I am powerless over alcohol. I will drive myself toward the comforts of senselessness if I dare take a mouthful. You will watch this change in confusion. But your bewilderment will not bother me, because I have already left you for something far more important. There is nothing I can do about that; remember, alcohol *always* wins.

I am powerless over alcohol. Its memory lingers, forever reminding me of the utter destruction I caused myself and those I love. I have finally come to understand where just one drink will take me, and why I can no longer follow its masterful suggestions. I have accepted what I must do in order to achieve this. I have openly surrendered my will to recovery so that I might live in the comfortable arms of serenity and everlasting peace.

Desperate Prayer
for Help

"Are you there God? Can you hear my voice? It's so muted now, I know. Something is wrong with me and I can't seem to stop it. I keep trying to call out to you. I'm guessing that you don't want to listen to me anymore. Where have you gone? How could you desert me like this? I'm in trouble and alone. You're all I have left. Perhaps you can't even save me now."

"Please, I'm begging you to rescue me! I'm really tired of this thing I keep doing. I think you know; you must. But, what is it? I don't understand. I know this is all my fault, and I deserve to be punished. I really tried today; I did, but I needed to have just one. Why are you keeping me in the dark? Oh God, I am scared because I can't stop. Oh God, I can't even imagine stopping. Could you at least tell me what is wrong with me?"

"It's true, you're avoiding me because all I ever do is mess things up. I swear that I don't mean to. Somehow, it just happens; sometimes, I can hardly remember it. I'm ashamed of myself for this persistent weakness. I can't figure out where it came from. There is an angry, evil spirit corrupting my soul, and you just don't care! Don't you see it? I'm right here, don't you know that? I'm failing; I'm falling. Aren't you supposed to heal the sick? Well, I'm sick; I'm shaken and wavering on madness. Doesn't that count?"

"No one understands me anymore; they have left me to rot. And not even my Almighty God can help me stop. Why aren't you listening to my pleas? I've lost my way. Can't you find the time to help me? How many more times do I have to say I'm sorry for yesterday? I'm so tired of apologizing for everything. I have tried so hard to stop causing problems. Something keeps taking me over, can't you see that?"

"I keep ruining everything I touch; I swear that I don't mean to. Can't you find any compassion for me? I can't stop, can't you see that? Yes, Your Honor, I am guilty for whatever this is. What is this? You are all I have left to hold on to. I'm on my knees. I can't stop, but I think I need to stop. I'm so horrified and scared."

"Where are you? I keep screaming, I keep screaming; I can't stop. I'm crawling on the ground like a slithering worm. I know that I'm dying, and yet, you are nowhere to be found. I can hear myself moaning, why can't you? Please, I will do anything for you if you could just make all this stop. I'm right here in the corner, trapped! Oh, please hurry, God. If you wait much longer, I'm afraid that you won't be able to find me. I'm willing to try anything if you could just make it stop."

Morning Coffee

I am awake, the sun is shining through the window, and I can remember everything I did yesterday. I am fully alive. I do not have a raging headache, nor am I running to the bathroom to let go of my insides. I feel healthy, and my skin is toned with color. My eyelids are not drooping. I can see myself clearly in the mirror.

I am sitting peacefully, enjoying my morning coffee, without the fear of recalling a disastrous moment. I can read the newspaper devoid of blurred vision. I am not running off to bed to heal myself from surmountable alcohol intake. I am only opening a bottle of refreshing orange juice. I'm frying an egg because I'm hungry. I'm not repulsed by the smell.

I'm happy because I can conquer a normal routine. I'm pleased with myself. These small pleasures give me strength and fulfillment. I am no longer undone. I am no longer stressed over forgetting or remembering. I'm solid. I'm okay, right now where I am. I'm organized. I'm able to work with an abounding ease. My calmed spirit within conveys a new sense of rhythm with a smile. I'm savoring this beautiful existence. I'm learning to use my newfound freedom in ways I never thought I could. I am real. I can feel this day, just for today. I am sober, and the world around me is filled with hope.

Disclosing a Drinking Problem

Okay, if I admit that I often drink too much, I'm going to have to go through the "I told you so" routine. I really don't like being minimized. If I give any inclination that I'm even processing these thoughts, they'll all clamor toward me with pamphlets of meaningless information which they miraculously "found" in their files. I really don't want to know that they've already researched this stuff.

Okay, let me rethink all of this one more time. If I tell them that I have concerns about my drinking patterns, they will automatically run around the house, tossing out every bottle of liquor. I don't think I'm ready for that kind of leap. Grimmer still, if I confess to even a hint of this, I will never be able to enjoy the pleasure of a buzz again. Ever. I really can't stand the thought of that.

Okay, if I even suggest that I am wondering about myself, everyone is going to be running over to have another one of those intervention powwow sessions again. They will inevitably do all the talking, while I sit there feeling a terrible sense of shame. I don't think I can deal with that embarrassment right now.

Okay, there's really nothing to think about here. I'm not going to miss out on a lifetime of fun and drinking just to please everyone else. They would be completely satisfied if I admitted to this kind of problem, now, wouldn't they? The "I told you so" grin would definitely be planted on their faces. Self-righteousness is definitely unbearable. Nope, not today anyway. I'm far better off by keeping my mouth shut. Maybe I'll try to concentrate on this dilemma again tomorrow. Right now, I could certainly use a drink.

Turning Left toward Tomorrow

I watched the cars pull out ahead of me. Each one had been waiting for the light to change on this dreary, rainy night. Every driver had attended the AA meeting and was heading home. As I waited behind them, I was suddenly struck by the moment, realizing that although we were all individuals, we were also individually suffering from alcoholism. We owned different cars, had different careers, and fought different problems, but we ultimately shared the same disease.

We had never known each other until we met in the fellowship. In the outside world, we were acquaintances and sometimes friends. We were separate in most things but still joined together with one common purpose: to stay sober for another day. Nobody would guess that we had just attended a meeting for this. The onlooker might watch the caravan of cars with no thought at all. They would never understand the mental anguish incurred by the alcoholic, nor would they notice any physical proof of it. Just a row of cars turning left at the light.

I wondered what the drivers were thinking. Did the meeting give them useful tools to face another day? Were they rehashing some of the insightful stories imparted by the man who once thought that drinking was the only way to operate his life? Were they inspired by the woman who managed to get through a year? Were they willing to believe that this form of encouragement could get them through that difficult time, when drinking sounds like the only thing to do? Were they contemplating tomorrow's routine, while mustering up the strength to actually make it through?

I could feel their pulse, as if it were my own. I knew this wasn't just a parade of cars rolling along the street on an ordinary night. These drivers were turning toward tomorrow with hope in hand, preparing to face another day, living without alcohol. This type of illness, this need for a drink, was something a normal person would never have to worry about. They might never fully understand what a meeting like ours meant to us, or how a group such as this counted on the strength of one another to maintain a sober life. I pressed on the gas with tears in my eyes, grateful that we could share a common problem in a safe haven, where honesty, understanding, and compassion set us free.

Excuses to Drink

"This was an unbearable day. I think I need a drink." "I just got the promotion. I truly deserve a drink." "How could my sister talk to me like that? I'll question her motives with a drink." "Vacation starts tomorrow. Let the festivities begin with a drink." "I can't stand the people I work with. A drink will help make me feel better." "I had a wonderful holiday. A drink will keep it going."

"I can't believe I wasted two hours on that stupid movie. Why not have a drink?" "I love basking in the sun! I'll make a drink to cool me down." "My spouse is irritating me tonight. A drink will help me lighten up." "My son got into college. I'll toast with a drink to his success." "There's always one more chore to do. A drink will make the day go faster." "I love being out with my friends. The drinks are on me."

"Everything went as planned. I'm worthy of a drink." "The car broke down again. I could really use a drink." "I won fifty dollars at poker. I'll celebrate with a drink." "My mother is making me crazy. My nerves could use a drink." "I jogged for the first time in years. I've earned a drink." "I'm just dead tired tonight. A drink will help me sleep." "Dinner was delicious. I'll have another drink while I clean up."

"My grandfather died. He would want me to commemorate him with a drink." "The weekend is almost here. Let's start it with a drink." "I was late for work again. A drink should calm me down." "I felt happy today. Why not keep my spirits up with a drink?" "The puppy did his business in the house for the second time this afternoon. I'll have a drink with the dog's training manual." "My boss gave me a compliment at lunch. This drink is warranted."

"I really have no reason to drink. I just need one." "I'm feeling under the weather this morning. Just one drink will fix me right up." "My hands keep shaking. A drink usually settles that down." "I just got sick on that last alcoholic concoction. Another drink will make it better." "I know I said that I would stick to coffee today. Perhaps I will just mix it with a drink." "I keep forgetting things. A drink will stir up my memory." "Nobody likes talking to me anymore. I guess I will have that drink alone." "I think I might have a drinking problem. Just one more drink before I quit."

Beginning of Sobriety

During my first eight weeks of sobriety, I lingered in the contentment of recovery. I clung to new awakenings, feeling physically better. I was somehow comforted by movies, a refreshing night's sleep, the tranquility of my home, a clearer mind, and the peace of normal living. These noticeable little freedoms astonished me and persevered my will for quite some time. The newness of becoming a human being again gave me resolve and purpose. I just felt good and was honestly surprised that everything was going so well. I thought for sure that I was a changed person who no longer had anything to worry about.

Suddenly, out of nowhere, my mood began to change. Sobriety became agitating. I hated having to be the alcoholic. I grew frustrated with everyone around me who could have a drink without life-threatening consequences. Jealousy reared its ugly head. For a short period of time, I chose to remain isolated from others. I wallowed in the stupidity of choosing to never drink again. I spent days focusing on all my growing irritations. I became wildly angry over the whole situation I had put myself in.

I questioned relapse. I pondered the notion of trying to

be a normal drinker. I envisioned the possibilities of becoming one. I paced the floor with uncertainty. I thought about all the angles of returning to alcohol. I screamed at God for allowing this disease to land on me. I raged at my unfortunate fate. I fell into the trap of self-pity with a howling pursuit. Nothing felt fair.

Somehow, I managed to get back on my knees to pray. I spit out my petitions with fiery tones and hostile complaints. My loud, anxious appeals echoed around me, while I begged for some sense of serenity. I wanted to stay sober; I *needed* to stay sober, but the whole process seemed momentarily overwhelming.

Apparently, my God was listening, because I found the strength to pull up my bootstraps and drive to an AA meeting. There, I expressed my nagging frustrations and challenges. I was heard without judgment. I learned that my crazy emotions were common to anyone new in sobriety. I walked away feeling understood and completely encouraged once more. A sense of relief permeated my spirit.

One meeting, a few fitful prayers, and a later call to my sponsor kept me away from that harrowing moment of total vulnerability when a drink seemed like the best solution. Emotions will waver; there will be some really bad days now and then. Remember, alcohol used to be the eraser, the calmer, and the absolute tool with which to survive. We've changed the substance and routine. And if we stick to the path of recovery, we will soon be astounded by the joys of sobriety and a life now well lived.

Ending It for Good

I am really going to do this today. I *have* to. I can't stand it anymore. I'm simply going to finish this bottle, maybe get another, and then get the courage to end this horrible reality. It's all there is to it. Nobody could possibly be living like this. I can't stand myself anymore. This whole thing is just too much for one person to take.

Oh my God, I'm so wasted again. I'm just going to bring the car in to the garage. Damn it, I have to move all this crap to the side in order to make room. Isn't it always something? One more swig while I figure this out. Why is there never space in here for a car? I'm really irritated. Can't anything simply go my way?

All right, I can do this. Just close the garage door, go get the key, put it in the ignition, and turn it. This won't take long; it's supposed to be fairly quick. Oh God, what if the carbon monoxide seeps into the house and kills the dog? I can't do that to him. He's been my only faithful friend. I know, I'll put him outside in the yard and have another drink. He'll be safe there in the fresh air.

Okay, settle down. You can do this. Stop worrying about the kids; they are old enough and are on their own now. They have their own lives. And hubby is about done with me anyway. The entire family is tired of me. People get over horrible events all the time and many of them have survived worse things than just suicide. Everyone gets dealt a bad hand. They will mend in due time, just turn the damn key.

I don't think I can do this to my children. Oh my God, I can't believe I'm really sitting here sobbing, ready to turn the car on. The dog is outside barking at something. What the hell am I doing? Somebody, please stop me! Where is everyone? What time is it? Why am I sweating so badly? Where am I?

I just can't do this today. What am I thinking? Get out of the car and pull it outside right now. This is madness. Stop crying and pull it together. Open the door and get out. This is getting scary. I'm actually terrified. Oh God, where are you? I'm stuck to the seat, and my hands are shaking. Somebody stop this confusion please.

Okay, calm down now, the car is outside. Was I having a nightmare? Did I *really* almost try that? Something is desperately wrong with me. I'm truly losing my mind. I'm seriously worried about myself! What should I do? These tears are putting me over the edge. I need to go in the house for a minute. Just breathe. Just breathe.

I've got the dog, and I'm just going to have to forget I even tried this stupid trick. Now, where did I put that bottle?

Our Silent Soldiers

There have always been those silent soldiers around us. The people who guarded our dignity somehow. Every alcoholic has at least one. They wear their dirty, frayed uniform each day without hesitation. They feel the weight of the additional armor that goes along with it, but they are willing to carry this burden. Their cumbersome role is to protect and defend the raging stranger they still live with, but no longer know. They diligently look after the fort with strength and fortitude. They do not budge from their resolve.

They stand and wait patiently. They rarely leave their post. Their eyes are fully focused on their position. They willingly safeguard what is left of the person burrowed deep within the fortress walls. And while they witness the suffering, they too suffer. As they hear the screams of hopelessness, they diligently linger with hope.

They learn to twist their thoughts in all directions. They know when to switch their position. The outside world is a place they can remember but no longer seek. They remain firm in their caretaking. They sacrifice and stay put. Their faces are etched in a stoic stance. They are aware that each day will be a challenge. They have come to accept this.

When the silent soldiers sleep, their dreams cry out for peace. They stir fitfully with little comfort. They are alone in their weeping. They rise again in duty with an early optimistic heart. They fervently believe in something; a chance that this stranger can be saved. They are confident in their faith. Their courage knows no boundaries.

There have always been silent soldiers around us. They gave shelter to our being, and they were intent on our survival. With sobriety, we finally come to realize that they were there all along. We spring forth toward them with an unending sense of gratitude. We are astounded by their strength and true dedication. We pay homage to their undying love and sacrifice. They stayed, so that we might get the chance to live again.

Glory Days

Football players like to recall their glory days with a nostalgic glow. Elderly people can revel in yesteryear with a bit of elaboration. Sometimes high school years can be remembered more fondly than they really were. Childhood stories often grow more exciting the older we get. People in general usually eulogize their past with a bit more adornment than is actually true. It is in our human nature to retell our tales with slightly altered memories. Time has the capability of changing long-ago recollections with an optimistic bent.

I can often fall into this trap of commemorating my drinking days with upbeat remembrances. Human nature likes to tell me that it wasn't all that bad. My alcoholic mind prefers to modify the devastating consequences of what really happened back then.

It's easy to go this route when you're teetering on having that drink. I'd like to tell myself that I was truly the life of the party way back when. It's fun to rewrite how I bought all those strangers fancy shots while making the crowd laugh. I can rework the entire evening of fanfare by ignoring the part when the bartender cut me off because I fell off the stool.

I can transform those days of continual drunks into

cherished, tranquil ones, deleting the part where I was passed out on the couch in front of the family. I can minimize that weeklong blackout by telling myself that I didn't miss a day on the job. The fact that I got fired weeks later had nothing to do with it. I can amend all those intoxicated conversations with eloquent reasoning. Erasing the part when I was slurring my words never has to be told.

I can talk up a story of how I could outdrink everyone around me. I can concoct a tall tale of admiration when my friends cheered over my stamina. Of course, omitting the part where I was dragged out to the car because I could barely stand up would have to ensue.

There are certain days when euphoric recall whispers in my ear. I can maximize the glory of my past and minimize the consequences. I can play pretend games and create new versions of what really occurred, thereby giving myself permission to drink again. But, if I am truly honest with myself when looking backward, I must accept the true reality. There were no glory days at all. I was never the life of the party. Usually, I was the death of it.

Physical Beating
by the Bottle

My body was physically wiped out by alcohol. The destruction was silently slow and insidious. As my drinking began taking its toll on me, I chose to ignore the obvious signs by opting for more. The bottle had a way of helping me erase my concerns, granting me reprieve from that nagging anxiety.

It wasn't unusual to wake up with a throbbing shoulder or leg. The difficulty was trying to remember how I'd done that the night before. It was apparent that I had fallen. I just couldn't recall the where or when. Most days I had to settle with a guess.

I knew things were getting worse when I could no longer cook without burning myself. I realized that I was definitely off balance when I blamed the dog's bowl for my three broken toes. I couldn't help but notice the persistent bruises on my body, which had no real reason to be there. I nervously worried when I began vomiting each morning. I fearfully accepted that the black eye wasn't there, because someone had punched me.

I slightly panicked when my liver and kidneys began to ache. I became somewhat tense with perpetual bladder infections. I knew I was not a pillar of health as I scrutinized my trembling hands. I apprehensively noted my deterioration when I looked in the mirror at a foggy-eyed, bloated, lifeless mess.

I allowed myself to buy just one more bottle, in order to ignore what I was truly seeing. I knew I was getting bad when this became my daily—and only—solution. I recognized that I was physically beaten when my mind consented to the severe consequences of this ritual. I accepted my alcoholic fate when I no longer cared about how my body was being battered by my justifications to drink.

Sober Introduction

It's fascinating how we get reintroduced to people we've already met once we're sober. In the beginning, it feels strange when our family and friends take great strides to show us off to other people. Their pride is sometimes overwhelming because we tend to remember our past, noting that we were not always the most respectable guest during previous events.

There is certainly good reason to be newly presented if we are honest with ourselves. A glimpse backward will help us remember how we were the inebriated disasters, who had far surpassed everyone else during cocktail hour. We often arrived with intoxicated momentum and courage. This whirling buzz gave us reckless assurances that we fit right in with the crowd. Our intentions were solely to behave and act well mannered, just like every normal drinker would. But in no time at all, we became the boisterous, self-seeking horn which ended up blowing out insults. People often rolled their eyes or shielded themselves from us. No doubt we hadn't noticed those reactions; the alcohol already had us believing that we were the life of the party.

Back then, we really thought that we were the stars of the show; the people everyone couldn't wait to be around.

Drinking allowed us to construct false bravado, even when we were blatantly causing commotion for everyone around us. Alcohol gave us the permission to fool ourselves into thinking that we were the best of the bunch.

In recovery, we are relaunched as new people who can finally share their true personalities and genuine worth. That fleeting moment of awkwardness will begin to pass when we realize that the people around us are truly embracing our amazing transformation. We have become new again, and as such, those who have always loved us want to share it.

I Drink like Everyone Else

"Give me a break, I'm just fine. There is nothing to be concerned about here. Are you kidding, look at all those other people ordering shots at the bar. That couple over there has already had a few glasses of wine. Do you think I didn't notice? Now that's funny. I saw that man with the red hat here the last time I was in. See, there's no problem. He likes this place too."

"Really, you're upset because I ordered one more for last call? Did you ever look at yourself in the mirror? Many other people drink doubles on the rocks. Please don't ruin my night by reminding me that you have to be the designated driver again. Are you seriously going to give me that same dissertation you gave last week before we went to the party?" "Did you ever watch your brother drink? Now, there's one with a problem. Half the family is a load of drunks anyway. My side might be worse, but they're all still alive and kicking. Now that's enough for me to go on. We've got those tolerant genes for sure. There is nothing to worry about."

"Please don't start an argument this morning. It's your friends' fault for buying us the last two drinks. *I'm* the one who wanted to go home, remember? Staying out that late has always made me tired, so forgive me if I need a nap already!"

"Let me remind you that I suggested the movies instead of the bar. Big deal, you know when to stop. Why are you complaining again? I warned you that I was in the mood to tie one on. Get over it; I'm stressed out beyond belief; that extra drink made me feel better. I'm about done with your guilt parade. Everyone else is out there partying just like me. Calm down, I'm just fine! There is nothing to be concerned about."

The Door Is Opening

The door is opening. Can you see the light shining through the crack? It's slowly flooding the room with all the hopeful possibilities you once had. It's reaching toward those dreams you once believed in. It's pulling you closer to the life you actually wanted.

Go ahead, turn that knob wider. Can you feel the stream of glowing miracles seeping onto where you stand? Are you absorbing the warmth of grace and peaceful anticipation? There is only optimism abounding. Embrace all your aspirations with bravery and longing.

Keep going now. Can you sense your desire for freedom? Are you becoming aware of all those future opportunities within it? This choice grants you permission to surrender those nagging fears which held you back and took you over. The miracle of healing is right in front of you.

Pull that door toward you. Are you noticing the gifts of mental clarity and confidence? Triumph, bravery, and victory await you. Your soul will be filled with rejoicing. From that will come vision, true desire, and independence.

You're almost there. Can you feel the light warming your spirit? Are you beginning to recognize that your past was only filled with darkness? You are witnessing sincere compassion and forgiveness. You are actually feeling again. Your body is slowly welcoming and remembering those real sensations.

You did it; you opened it wide. Can you sense the soothing essence of the light? Are you being quieted now in the hands of serenity? Is your heart suddenly beating with courage and hope? You are brimming with the happiness of a life rich in the energy of determination and strength. A light only captured by surrendering to the power of recovery.

I Can't Go Back Again

I just don't want to go back there again. Today, I realize that I was not living at all. I am astounded when I remember myself as that suffering human being who clung to a bottle amidst the shadowy shame of total intoxication. Sometimes I can't believe that I lasted as long as I did trying to manage what was left of my world, while prioritizing my need to drink. If nothing else, that game was exhausting.

I just don't want to go back there again. I shudder with nervousness when I recall how the despondency and hopelessness overpowered my days. I can almost feel my hands shake as they once did while I tried desperately to control them. The emotional weight I dutifully carried makes me wonder how I survived such persistent insanity. I had been a bedraggled entity taunted by fear and guilt, always grasping for another drink to make it all go away.

I just can't go back there again. Past recollections show me all the reasons why I must never return. I had willingly filed myself away, far beyond reach and recognition. My commitment to alcohol unwittingly surpassed the needs of those I loved. The daily remorse burned my spirit, causing me to fall deeper into necessary unconscious living. I went as far as finally wishing for death.

I just can't go back there again. My old, shiftless memoir describes the incessant, troubled madness of my routines. It portrays the muddled hourly panic of knowing that my actions no longer resulted in good outcomes. It defines a life of fear, anxiety, and utter grief.

I just can't go back there again because I have become a human being once more. I am no longer a captive of oppression, nor a slave to the lies of what daily drinking promised. I have been freed of its bondage, walking peacefully in the land of the living.

Learning to Forgive

When I was drinking, being forgiven or forgiving someone else was about the last thing on my mind. I had no intention whatsoever to bow down to anyone. If they couldn't reconcile with my mistakes, than that was their problem.

In my swirling mind, I had no obligation to forgive all those people who once hurt me. In fact, it was their actions which had caused me to gulp down alcohol so incessantly. The idea of letting these individuals be pardoned for their misdeeds was out of the question. And for another thing, I didn't need absolution; I wasn't doing anything wrong.

The idea of cowering before forgiveness made me want to recoil. I thought that the whole "I am so sorry" theory never solved any dilemma. All the trouble challenging my life was entirely due to the fact that everyone was always minimizing my self-worth. If anyone needed to be exonerated, it was *me*.

Those were my thoughts when the bottle ran my life. I was absolutely certain that any form of atonement could not be attained. There was a serious mess to clean up, and a pile of mistakes far too numerous to be set free. Amending anything seemed exhaustingly overwhelming.

Recovery has led me to a quite different scenario. It has

taught me to understand and accept that we humans often cause pain unintentionally. What I might have perceived to be a mean-spirited action by another may not have been their aim. Or if their desire was to hurt me, then I have to resolve the issue within myself. Harboring any kind of resentment only resulted in furthering my own heartache.

I found that disliking another for whatever reason only made me feel worse. I didn't need to sit in this kind of perplexing anger any longer. The only solution was to forgive and move forward. This miracle of release began to free my soul from within. I discovered a peaceful grace in my life when I chose absolution. I have rid myself of all these burdens, which, in turn, have given me the courage to maintain a life filled with serenity and love.

Intervention

Some people have a lot of nerve, politely asking me to sit down in my own house. It's so frustrating to watch how they purposely surround me in some idyllic holy formation. I've witnessed this whole thing before. In just a few minutes, somebody is going to start with their list of concerns for my well-being. In my mind, I can already see myself screaming, "Are we *really* going to have this same, stupid discussion again? Quite frankly, I am plain tired of it."

Well, the only thing I can do now is try to look comfortable as I listen to their self-righteous blabbing. I'll nod my head toward their every word. I'll tell them that I will start watching what I drink. I will wholeheartedly apologize for my little mistakes…and then I'll run to the store for some liquor when they're finished. I guess I can handle this silly powwow for a few minutes.

Thank God that's finished. Nothing like having to suck it up and act as if I'm grateful for all their concern. I've got my bottle now, and I can get back to reality. Seriously, though, they sure had a lot of gall, talking to me like that. Of course, they're the sort who do *everything* perfectly. They find pleasure in reminding me that the way I live isn't up to their standards. Hell, I've seen them drinking too; they're no better than I am when they party it up. And all that sappy melodrama about how I have all these talents which I am supposedly not using is about enough to make me pack up and leave. I know there are people out there who might give me a little more respect!

The more I consider all of their petty, unjustified tirades, the more I want to drink. I'll finish this whole bottle if I have to. Why can't everyone leave me alone? If they would only let me live how I want to live, we wouldn't have to have these "do-gooder sit-downs" in the middle of the afternoon. Honestly, they are really making me crazy!

Here's a thought…Maybe if they stopped dumping guilt on me, I wouldn't be this angry. If they had to deal with the things *I* have to deal with, they might have a few more drinks too. I am *always* the one who has to handle every single thing, while they selfishly promote their own agendas. Why can't they see that? I know they're far too self-absorbed to consider any of my points.

Well, my little friends, let it be known right now that I will no longer tolerate your mercenary, small-minded chats. How dare you critique *my* mistakes when *you* have plenty of your own! Be reminded that I am not some doomed psychotic who needs to be analyzed for every drink I take. Go examine your own lives and leave me out of it! Now, where did I put that bottle?

I Could No Longer...

I could no longer endure my suffering. I could no longer wake up with the shame of my daily living. I could no longer tolerate the suffocation of my ever-present guilt. I could no longer withstand the cruelty of my disease. I could no longer bear the physical beatings every morning. I could no longer tolerate my obsession with the bottle. I could no longer face my ever-growing fears.

I could no longer convince those who loved me that everything was okay. I could no longer focus on normal routines. I could no longer feel the presence of the world. I could no longer stomach my wretched appearance. I could no longer brave the hopelessness. I could no longer fail the family I loved. I could no longer accept my continued mistakes. I could no longer linger in total isolation.

I could no longer find comfort in hiding. I could no longer measure out the length of my days. I could no longer put up with my twisted mind. I could no longer continue to tell myself that I was all right. I could no longer deal with the grief surrounding me. I could no longer convince myself that tomorrow would be different. I could no longer latch on to a purpose.

I could no longer sustain my desire to drink. I could no

longer be the figure of ridicule and contempt. I could no longer drive myself to do anything. I could no longer stop my continued weeping. I could no longer harbor my fits of anger. I could no longer wake to yet another day of sordid emptiness. I could no longer live this tragedy. I could no longer spend another minute in remorse. I could no longer antagonize another human being. I could no longer speak with any authority. I could no longer trace my yesterdays. I could no longer sit in comfort. I could no longer hunger for a way out of this. I could no longer officially state that I was living. I could no longer dismiss the reality of my alcoholism.

Amazing Sense of Peace

I found an amazing sense of peace once I embraced my Higher Power, who I call God. Before alcohol over took my life, I was fairly spiritual and religious. My faith in something else other than myself prevailed then. But as I lunged myself further into the bottle, I gave up on any meaningful commitment to my God.

I felt forgotten and forsaken. There were nights when I drunkenly begged to be saved from my hopelessness and despondency. Admittedly, this became my mundane ritual before inevitably pouring that first drink. I pleaded with my God to remove it from my hands, but somehow, I wound up intoxicated every time. Frustrated and alone, I came to believe that no one was listening. I conceded that faith was a man-made notion, and I would have to try to solve my own drunken mess.

Since then, I have come to believe once more. The God of my understanding is with me. He always was; I just preferred to ignore him then. I have surrendered my will to my Higher Power, so that I won't have to go it alone. I am no longer in charge. This freeing concession has renewed my soul, enabling me to walk forward in strength.

I seek daily prayer and meditation. I have confessed my

past mistakes to God and my sponsor. I have made amends to those I have deeply hurt. I could never have found the courage to face these difficult milestones alone without this form of surrender. I can feel his presence in all my daily activities. I can feel his protection when I have the urge to drink. Most of all, I know that he is always there with me, pushing me forward unto a sober future where life is meaningful and free.

Alcohol Financially Corrupts

Alcohol financially corrupted me. I incurred court costs, legal fees, and fines because of my exploits with the law. My insurance premiums skyrocketed after my DUI, affecting my entire family. I managed to amass unreasonable bar tabs due to my drunken desire to buy all my newfound friends a drink. These stunning totals with overly generous tips piled up on my credit card.

I incurred countless hospital bills due to my continued falls and self-induced ailments notoriously caused by my drinking habits. I purposely skipped over bills when I didn't feel like facing them. I accrued late charges for missed payments far too often. I routinely spent money on fast food and other magical potions to relieve hangovers. Withdrawing cash from the ATM machine became a daily routine since my bottle of booze always seemed to evaporate. It didn't seem to bother me if I was using up the overdraft protection specifically meant for *real* banking issues, nor did I care about the ongoing fees related to this problem.

Extra shots were always in order when I was playing the "life of the party" role. Top-shelf liquor was a must during these happy events. My silly whims and unreasonable cravings continually gave way to an extremely hefty price. I never found time to review all the job opportunities available to me. I lost out on ample prospects who offered desirable paychecks because I preferred to drink instead. I spent cash on needless items as I wandered through the stores, trying to focus on something other than alcohol.

I rang up every reason to bring extra bottles of wine to the party. I filled the cabinets with aspirin and other medicines to heal my ailing body. The endless visits to the counselors put a dent in our insurance claims. Adding value to a savings account was the least of my concerns. The cost of rehabilitation was never a budget item; it eventually took the place of a family vacation—and more.

Alcohol financially corrupted me. My disease consumed any productive cash flow without regard for substantive consequences. It dissolved any normal behavior belonging to reasonable economic security. It plunged me into shady and dishonest acts. When drinking became the only priority of mine, wasting money meant keeping myself wasted. Prospective opportunities at maintaining a well-balanced accounting of my life had been tainted, and in the end, the price was financially striking.

Recovery Comes First

I know it's hard for you to understand me now. I think you might slightly miss some of the good old times we had together. You may even be wishing that I was still sitting next to you at the bar. And then again, maybe not. I recognize that sometimes you find it safer to avoid me, because I can no longer drink. I grasp that you still can without the same kind of consequences I have racked up. I get that you want me to tag along, but I can also feel the distance between us because of my own concerns. I am fully aware of your feelings. I know that it's rather difficult to accept this abrupt, overwhelming change. For years, we could thoughtlessly merry-make without a care in the world. But I can't run with that crowd anymore. Right now, I simply can't take those chances. Saying "no" to you is not a negative reflection of our friendship; it only means that my recovery has to come first.

I'm sorry for the past few times when I left you at the party. My desire to drink was far outweighing the fun we were having together. Slipping away secretly was the only way out.

Our road together has been altered. We are both learning how to adjust. I want you to know that I realize how much my recovery affects you. I also know that you truly understand how much I needed it.

Believe me, there are moments when I waver, wishing I didn't have to do this. But I can't drink like you, I can't stop like you, and I can't behave like you when I have just one. I've come to accept this reality. I hope that you can appreciate this, because you have seen me at my worst. My only request is that you bear with me for a little while longer.

I respectfully ask that you give me a little room to figure out this new life, and a little understanding when I have to say "no." I am healing and learning. Eventually, I will be strong enough to rejoin you in the world once more. Please understand that recovery is a process. Right now, it has to come first.

Something Is Definitely Wrong with Me

Something is definitely wrong with me; there just has to be. Nobody else in the world could possibly be hiding bottles of liquor in secret places around the house. I mean, who goes about their day thinking about buying the next bottle of booze? Who else could possibly be running to the store to buy more alcohol to pour into the household bottles, making it look like they hadn't drunk from them the night before? This just can't be normal.

Something is definitely wrong with me. Who walks around the grocery store avoiding the wine aisle the whole time, only to grab a few bottles at the last minute? Who could honestly be buying one bottle of white wine for the family refrigerator, and then a few extra ones to stash away for personal use? This just can't be right.

Something is definitely wrong with me. First, people don't hide bottles, and second, if they do, they at least know where they put them. Not only am I hiding them, now I'm forgetting where I stored them. I'm spending far too much time searching for this kind of nonsense. Who even does this kind of thing? This can't be natural.

Something is definitely wrong with me. Who, out there, could conceivably be worried about drinking all the time? I don't even think alcoholics are as focused on it as much as I am. Clearly, I seem to be the only person in the room who gets irritated when there is only coffee being served. This just can't be reasonable thinking.

Something is definitely wrong with me. I see people out all the time having a few cocktails, and then stopping. Why am I sneaking drinks on the other side of the bar so they won't see me? Who else is slyly gulping down covert glasses of double shots of vodka? Nobody else is doing this sort of thing. This just can't be typical behavior.

Something is definitely wrong with me. Nobody else is drunk before parties and totally wasted after them. Who out there decides to pump up with alcohol hours before an event? I can't imagine that there are other human beings on the face of the planet who mull over this kind of stuff. This can't be ordinary thinking.

Something is definitely wrong with me. More than a million different times I have forgotten what I have done the night before. Who else could actually be waking up most mornings with this kind of memory loss? Nobody else drinks into oblivion. Nobody else has to remind themselves to stop. This can't be anybody else's daily routine.

Something is definitely wrong with me. Nobody else is drinking, only me. Not one person out there can drink bottle after bottle like me. Who in God's name would be doing any of this except me? Is anybody else asking themselves if they drink too much? Nobody but me! This is clearly irrational thinking. Something is definitely wrong with me!

A Participant in My Own Life

I am a participant in my own life now. I remember what happened yesterday, and I have some idea of how tomorrow might be spent. I can concentrate on my work without the thud of a headache. I arise each morning with clarity, assured that I did not pass out again last night.

I am a participant in my own decisions because my brain is actually aware of what is going on around me. I can exercise with a determined energy rather than sulking on a couch. I have the ability to succinctly follow a routine without worrying about buying a bottle.

I am a participant in friendships today. I no longer have to hide from them. I attend events without fear of slurring my words. I am capable of creating new relationships because I am beginning to like myself once more. I am free from self-loathing. I have become a person with a personality. I have grown comfortable in my own shoes.

I am a participant in my family again. I soundly show up for every gathering where I am welcomed and loved. I can face little aggravations without drinking, and I can face the big ones as well. I honor schedules and most expectations. I am no longer reminded of my past mistakes. I feel the presence of happiness. I have dealt with most of my sorrows.

I am a participant in real living. I cook without burning myself like I once did. I am no longer consistently tripping over my feet. I can chat with the neighbors without smelling like booze. I can attend to the laundry and clean the house when I should.

I am a participant in my own personal freedom from alcohol. I am focused on what needs to be done each day in recovery. I am willing to do the work. I have made sober friends who help me stay focused. I use every tool possible to maintain this productive life where I am capable of participation and growth.

Problems Are a Part of Living

I am a recovering alcoholic who still has many of the same problems I often had when I was drinking. That is not going to change. But with sobriety comes the ability to sift through various challenges with a clear mind and honest approach. Hardballs have been thrown my way at the most inopportune times. People often don't do as I wish. Most of the time, I do not always get my way. Occasionally, my opinions are challenged. Once in a while, I am seen and not heard.

My plan is not necessarily someone else's. Other people's decisions don't always make me happy. There are moments when I discover lingering resentments from my past. Some weeks aren't always as peaceful as I'd like them to be. Anxiety and worry can still rear their ugly heads when I least expect it. Reality has proven that daily routines do not always go as planned.

Today, I am able to figure out how to deal with natural stumbling blocks, which are a part of everyday life. My healing brain is absorbing real emotion, minus the perplexity of intoxication. I can face ordinary obstacles with a new brand of thinking; only this time, sanity rules my awareness. I am no longer pointing fingers at anyone else, nor am I crafting half-truths and blown-up projections of what I think I perceive. I am conquering these issues in a normal state of being.

Just like anyone else, I get mad, feel pain, and sigh with frustration. My emotions may waver, but my well-balanced behavior usually prevails. My valid feelings are duly noted by others, and I get to experience the consideration of my feelings. Sobriety helps me to apply sound reasoning as I deal with life's problems head-on. I have learned to seek goal-driven results by solving dilemmas with rational, sober thinking.

It Wasn't Easy at First

Newly sober, everything I did was a battle. Unfamiliar with every aspect of recovery, my first focus was on not taking that drink. There were plenty of places I had to avoid, even in my own home. My thoughts wavered from feeling the desire to have just one, to that momentous contentment of rational thinking. In fact, there were times when I questioned which result was more preferable. I was a total melting pot of quivering emotion.

In the beginning, even the smallest chores tested my resolve. It wasn't easy going to the grocery store, where aisles of wine and beer beckoned my name. Errands meant passing by that place where I once bought my liquor. The old hiding spots in my home where I had previously stashed my bottles led me to remorseful thinking. Meaningless sunny afternoons suggested that picking up a cocktail was in order. Friends stopping by to visit signified that I should naturally have a drink.

In the beginning, each part of my life was questioning me. I had spent so many years boozing it up, that normal activities seemed almost strange. Talking on the phone without drinking, maintaining the home without drinking, getting ready for a party without drinking simply didn't feel natural.

In the beginning, it was a daily challenge to adhere to this huge lifestyle change. I was constantly fighting the urge to return to the world where I had been accustomed to living. Every now and then, I deliberated with myself, weighing the options of drinking again. My mind was running amok with deception, which took every ounce of energy to control.

In the beginning, remaining sober was a poignant battle. Courage and strength became necessities. I came to understand that I had to face this reality head-on. Life itself was streaming toward me on its own terms. Living in the real world meant living without the one coping mechanism which had failed me far too many times.

They're Watching Me

All right, I know they're watching me. Time to paste on that sober face and stop slouching. Go on, order that Coke and ask for an ice water too. There, that helps a bit. Think, think, move that brain to normal conversation. Best to keep this discussion light; they're asking me to repeat what I just said. Jeez, I just mispronounced my friend's name. I think I'd better run off to the bathroom to save face. I might want to splash some cold water on it too. Okay, pull yourself together, breathe a bit. Steady thoughts; mind your manners, and act normal. You can do this; you've done it before. By the time you get back out there, they'll have forgotten all about you. Ease into it, and then grab just one more Coke before you order that next drink.

I'm looking good, and they seem to be ignoring me right now. Perfect timing to slide myself to the other side of the bar where I can grab a quick double. Maybe I'll have the bartender slip it into my Coke glass. Now that's the kind of idea I can count on all night. I'm back in action, and no one is noticing a thing.

It's been over an hour since I bought a drink in front of them. I'm sure they will all be in agreement with that. I'll buy a round for everyone. That way, everything looks good. This is great; they're truly enjoying themselves, and I'm fitting right in. All have to do is act like I'm needing the restroom again and get one more double. I can use the excuse about having all those Cokes running through my system.

Why is everybody staring at me? I can't believe I just fell off the barstool. My drink is all over the floor, and I'm sopping wet. Here goes the sermon again, and now they're dragging me out the door. Why does this always have to happen to me when they're around? It wasn't like I had that much to drink. Well, the party's over, and they're going to make sure of it. I'd better have a good explanation on how this happened this time; otherwise, tomorrow is going to be filled with sanctimonious preaching and concern. Next time, I think I'd better drink a few more Cokes.

Facing the Past

Once I discovered that I was a real human being who could actually operate a life without alcohol, I began feeling pangs of sorrow. I loved being normal, but I hated that constant nudging regret of not having chosen sobriety years before. I could have had this good life a long time ago, and it bothered me.

I spent bitter days lingering in remorse. I reminded myself that I really could have done without the chaos. Beautiful memories might have been made, instead of drinking my existence away. I recognized that I had truly messed up some promising opportunities. I admonished myself for not opting for a sober life sooner. My heart ached for everything I had squandered.

For quite some time, I allowed this despondent thinking to prevail. I managed to fall back down into the pit of isolation, only this time I wasn't drinking. I turned down invitations to be with people. I filled my mind with negativity and defeat. I didn't want to share my sadness with anyone, nor did I want to wake up with that bouncing energy I had claimed only weeks before. My losses nagged at my soul, and they didn't want to release me.

Finally, I couldn't tolerate my blurred thinking anymore. I

understood that I had one of two choices to make. The first would allow me to opt for the unfaithful comfort of the bottle, whereby I could live in a muffled dream state of forgetting. I would be blissfully content in unconscious living. I would be able to shelve all these hauntings for another day. But with it came shame, guilt, and a new list of losses to resolve. Did I *really* want to start over again?

The next choice was to accept the grace of sobriety. Should I select this avenue, I knew that I would have to come to terms with my past. I would have to dispose of the "what-ifs" and accept the "what-is." I would have to challenge myself to face these disappointments head-on. Then, I would have to let go of these regrets unconditionally.

I paused to add up the consequences of taking that drink versus the results of remaining in recovery. The answer was simple: Sobriety was the only route to take, and I didn't want to squander any more time. I progressively tackled my innermost demons through the help of my sponsor and the steps of the AA fellowship. In time, the hopeless pain of my past was replaced by the commitment to make new, happy memories... one day at a time.

Liquid Mind of Encouragement

Day after day, I would pour my desperation into the bottle, giving it the permission to rehabilitate my continual negative thinking. It was the necessary requirement in facing all the haunting echoes of my past. The buzz amended my unreasonable fears. It helped me ignore the incessant nagging voice, which constantly reminded me of how bad I really was.

This kind of chronic forgetting let me move right along in my life without consequence. It allowed me to become the person I had always wanted to be, granting me the nerve to view myself differently. I was the mighty warrior, strong and invincible. I was accomplished in all things. I applauded my achievements, and I prided myself in being better than anyone else. My liquid mind encouraged me in a way nobody else could

When I wasn't drenching myself with alcohol, on those tough days when my body needed a break, I found that I wasn't any of those things the bottle had been tantalizing me with. I couldn't seem to focus on that impressive individual who seemed so real when I was drinking.

The terrible fact lashed out before me; I wasn't successful

at all. I had only become a pathetic, sick human being who could barely get in a day's work. Worse than that, the only thing I could give myself credit for was making it through a twenty-four-hour period without a drink.

I could hardly face this truth, and I didn't know how to resolve this glaring snag. I felt overwhelmingly alone. I was convinced that no one could ever understand my plight nor my frantic need to keep my drinking ritual intact. I thought that my problem was unsolvable. I was totally certain that there was no way out. The only thing left to do was to return to my liquid mind of encouragement where I would find solace in my own insanity, a place which gave me permission to pretend.

Cold Shoulder

As usual, my loving family is purposefully eyeballing me this morning. Of course, they're trying to subtly point out that I did it again. This crew is on the muscle every single day; it's becoming apparent that they are not going to change their attitude. Unfortunately, I can't quite remember exactly what I did last night, so it looks like I'm going to have to figure it out on my own. Sure, I had a few customary drinks. Plenty of people do that after a long day. It certainly isn't that uncommon. It's too bad that they can't understand that.

Well, I am obviously being ignored. Honestly, this kind of behavior is really unacceptable. In about one minute, I'm going to start screaming something like, "Just come out with it and stop playing mind games!" But I'm really in no mood to start some overblown argument where they end up speaking to me self-righteously. Plus, I can't stand those ridiculous, exaggerated lectures. It's not worth it in the end.

Darn, I despise this silly tiptoeing around the house stuff in order to keep them all happy. It's really not fair that they get to run this show. No matter what I do, nobody is ever satisfied! If anyone else knew what I had to live with around here, they would truly empathize with my side of things. Dwelling in a home with impeccable people would make anyone nuts. This constant cold shoulder routine is beginning to make me crazy. I absolutely hate when the day goes this way. I'm starting to wonder if they think it's humorous to disregard my presence. Seriously, it's similar to playing hide-and-seek. Well, I am more than happy to slip into another room anyway. I could use some quiet relief from all this debilitating edginess poured out on me all the time.

Yes, it would certainly help if I could recall part of my day yesterday. Evidently, I have some kind of problem to solve. But it would be nice if somebody gave me a little hint, now, wouldn't it? After all, we do cohabitate under the same roof! Well, I know that's not going to happen since they love to keep me guessing. This is our family tradition, our ongoing ritual; why would it change? It really doesn't matter; I have grown accustomed to their alienation. I ought to be used to it by now.

That said, I guess the best thing for me to do is to go about my business, all the while proving to them that I have no interest in their cold shoulder parade. The second-best thing to do is to run to the liquor store as soon as I can. A few drinks always helps me figure out this kind of puzzling situation. It's a real benefit under these circumstances. If nothing else, at least I'll feel better. If I were treated like a real human being around here, I wouldn't be forced into always having to go this route!

It's a Miracle

It's a miracle! I'm sober again today! Never in my wildest imagination did I think this could happen. If you would have told me this time last year that I would be free from alcohol, I would have laughed in your face. I would have mocked you with utter contempt. I would have called you a liar.

It's a miracle! I am actually living each day without drinking. I am not constantly consumed by its pull. Only months ago, I thought I was dying. But I have actually returned to a life. My family and friends are happier now because I have stayed true to recovery. Everyone is smiling.

It's a miracle! I awoke this morning feeling exuberant. I wasn't washing away last night's memory with alcohol. I didn't get sick, nor did I shake. I am busy with what needs to be done on this day. I have the ability to write lists and execute them with a sense of pride. Drinking no longer interferes with my progress.

It's a miracle! I never dreamed that I could find joy in normal living. I am physically part of the world where I once was an isolated victim clinging to a bottle. I am aware of my own needs and the needs of others. That focus on daily drinking is no longer encompassing my plans. I am shockingly free from the clutches of that mesmerizing intoxication.

It's a miracle! I never believed that I could actually be helped. That lost soul buried in desperation and futility has changed. I have been rescued and discovered. I am mentally capable of pursuing my dreams. I no longer inhabit that realm of wishful thinking. I can achieve whatever I put my rational mind to.

It's a miracle! I am sober again today! I am happy and fulfilled by every sound step I take. I am walking in the light, and I can feel its rays touching my being. I have a very important place now, in the land of the living. I am human once more. I am an astounding wonder. I am a thriving miracle, who never thought this could actually happen.

The AA Meeting

You can't imagine the real relief I felt the first time I went to an AA meeting. Somehow, I felt a surge of freedom when I finally proclaimed that I was an alcoholic. In one split second, I was comfortable in a room where there were other people in the world, just like me.

This awakened liberation was powerful. I was actually sitting among other human beings who had also drowned their own lives in a bottle. There was no judgment or scorn. Nobody was laughed at or berated for admitting how badly alcohol had ruined their lives. Ridicule and contempt were nonexistent.

I gained ardent supporters who would do almost anything to help me maintain my recovery. I was happily floored by the well-wishing and creative hints meant to keep me going, one day at a time. Mere strangers offered their numbers, in case I needed a sober friend to talk to. Resounding words of encouragement exploded around me. I was never mocked for admitting that I was one of those who hid bottles around the house; many of them had done it themselves. People empathized with my disastrous past as if they had lived it themselves.

The group roared with applause when someone announced that they had made it through yet another month, or year, or day, without drinking. Arms were opened to any individual who had slipped back into the bottle but wanted another chance. There was no such thing as conviction; the quiet understanding of compassion seemingly prevailed. Everyone shared that common thread of alcoholic suffering.

You can't imagine what if felt like to be relieved of the bondage, which I once thought was only mine. The moment I arrived, I instantly knew that I was no longer alone. Every unfamiliar face, from all walks of life, made me feel safe in mere seconds. I was welcomed like an old friend who had finally belonged.

The Hungover Procedure

Oh, how I hated those hungover mornings, lying under the damp sheets soaked with sweat. My yellowed eyes would open, and I just knew what I needed to prepare for. My daily ritual was already beginning. The process was an ugly one, and I had grown accustomed to it.

My standard procedure went as follows:

1. Close your eyes for a little longer.

2. Open them, look at the clock.

3. Figure out what you did last night.

4. Calm yourself down because you already know it wasn't good.

5. Sift through the problems you caused.

6. Develop a plan to get yourself out of them.

7. Take a drink of water by the bedside.

8. Muscle up the nerve to move into the bathroom.

9. Fill the toilet with vomit.

10. Tell yourself that you will not drink today.

11. Drink more water.

12. Beat yourself up in the shower and beg for forgiveness.

13. Look at your bloated face in the mirror with shame.

14. Muster the strength to make coffee.

15. Sit and watch your shaking hands.

16. Remind yourself that today you will not go out and buy a bottle.

17. Eat a piece of toast for energy.

18. Review your situation once more.

19. Do a few chores to get your mind off of it.

20. Speak soundly to your soul that something is really wrong.

21. Make some reasonable excuses as to why this is happening.

22. Begin to worry about how insane you have become.

23. Fret over the entire way you are living.

24. Determine that you need to find a way to forget.

25. Resolve this issue by finding your hidden bottle.

26. Ease into unconscious shelving of your worries.

27. Drink whatever you have left.

28. Go to the store for more.

29. Whittle away the hours into oblivion and a sense of safety.

Understand that you will inevitably do the same thing again tomorrow.

Forgiving Yourself
for This Disease

During the first few weeks of sobriety, I could barely face the shame and guilt brought on by my disastrous drinking days. I was consumed by the unbearable recollection of the terrible harm I had done to everyone around me. Day after day, I would beat myself up for all the problems I had caused for those I loved. My mind solely recognized the painstaking sacrifices my family and friends had made during those daunting years. With clear eyes, I could see the ramifications of my chaotic, destructive life. Almost daily, some little thing would trigger a terrible memory of how I had treated the people I loved while under the influence of alcohol.

The grief surrounding my past actions was overwhelming until I finally accepted the fact that alcoholism is a disease. I was a human being dealing with a terrible affliction; one that was made to create a monster out of me. My brain was wired differently from others who were normal drinkers. The plain truth was evident; I could not stop after one drink and my body adversely processed my alcohol intake. I had an illness that could only be cured by never drinking again.

Once I finally came to terms with the truth, that my pursuit of the bottle was an actual scientifically proven malady, I was then able to slowly ease into forgiving myself for my past actions. I learned to recognize that my desire to drink wasn't due to some immoral defect or weakness. I was simply a person whose brain couldn't handle alcohol normally.

I tackled old memories with an altered viewpoint. There, I was able to admit to my part of the problem in a past event, then absolve myself for the role my alcoholism also played in it. Day by day, serenity slowly seeped in, opening the door to forgiveness and peace of mind.

Feeling Edgy in Recovery

Today I feel edgy in recovery. Nope, I have no desire to take a drink, but there is that little devil on my shoulder nudging me in the Wrong direction. I am not really obsessing about it, but for some reason I feel like I am. It's just a beautiful day outside, and my mind is telling me that I ought to celebrate it! The best way to enjoy the outdoors is to have something soothing to go along with it. Alcohol is the only thing which seems to makes sense. It's easy to remember my past escapades in weather like this. I am aware of it. I feel its pulse. The memories are right around the corner, and I must stop them immediately.

I am definitely edgy; I feel the battle brewing in my head. I can't help but consider my options. I am envisioning that magical liquid flowing down my throat. I feel my senses dissolve into an unconscious freedom while the sunlight pours down onto my face. I experience the lightness of being caressing my eyelids. The vast release of the world where worries and problems no longer bind me sound suddenly intriguing. I revel in my thinking, and for a moment, I am caught in the cunning snare of my past.

I am edgier still because my endless thoughts are nagging me. The real truth is not what I seemingly want it to be.

Slipping away on a gorgeous afternoon only led to tumultuous evenings where my intoxication grew into arguments, isolation, and shame. The unconscious freedom never lasted, and my body only craved more of it. My mind is alerted to the fact that I am playing a make-believe game with myself. I never really witnessed those beautiful days. Instead, I spent them whiling away in blackouts.

As I begin to realize that my brain is playing tricks on me, I come to terms with my edginess. I have to take hold of it somehow, or it will win that piece of me still conquering addiction. I know that I cannot sit on the edge in this way. The feeling is a dangerous one. My recovery will fail should I continue to contemplate this path.

There is another way to take the edge off. There is another choice to choose. I gather my will, I push my insane notions aside, and I simply make that call to another alcoholic. Within minutes, a voice of reason is speaking to me. Words of understanding and hope comfort me across the line. I feel the edgy prodding of my very soul slip away. This relief absorbs my mind, and I am able to walk outside once more feeling the freedom of the great outdoors and the courage to remain sober.

Nightmare

"I had a terrible nightmare last night. I dreamed that you and I had come home from dinner, only to find a roaring party going on there. I decided to run down to the basement and check on things. The place was filled with strangers dancing to loud music, while holding large mugs of beer in their hands. I didn't recognize a single soul, and I began shouting at them. All of a sudden, it occurred to me that I had left you upstairs. Total fear encompassed me as I ran up the steps".

"My heart beat with an awful memory of long-ago parties, when you could hardly stand up. By the time I got to the kitchen, you were already washed away with intoxication, glaring at me with those unbearable, emptied eyes. I cried out for you, but you could no longer look my way. Tears gushed down my face like a torrential rainfall. I couldn't muffle my agonizing sobs. You were gone again, and I knew it. Only this time, I was even more afraid that I might never get you back."

A loved one shared this painful dream with me. His portrayal of my inebriated state and his concerns for my well-being revealed that even in sound recovery, he still worried about the day when I might opt for a drink. At that moment, I realized how my alcoholism had affected those who loved me. It made clear that my sobriety is still often on their minds.

Sometimes as we begin to make great strides in our recovery, we tend to forget about those who had always been by our side. Remember them? The people who: put us to bed, brought us water when we were sick, prayed every night that we might survive another day, defended our mishaps, picked us up at the police station, carried on with the chores, declined invitations on our behalf, lied about our drinking, valued our humanity, calmed all of our storms, and maintained our dignity if they could.

They also labored in our darkness, and they are as much a part of our recovery as we are. They are surviving and changing right along with us. We must come to accept their anxious feelings at a party or their need to safeguard our sobriety, even if it feels smothering. Remember, there was a time when that nightmare was all too real.

The Laundry

The clothes in the washer smell moldy. Looks like they have been sitting in there for a few days. Where did I hide that vodka? I think I cleaned the bathrooms yesterday, but I'd better check to make sure they look all right. Now, did I stash that bottle in between the mattress last night? I really need to make the effort to look like I've done something around here today. Well, here's the bottle; I guess I thought the linen closet was a better place to put it.

I think I'll dust this bedroom. I can't quite recall when I last cleaned in here. Just one swig will give me the energy to get this project done. Not too bad; this room looks formidable now. I've earned another sip! I should probably vacuum the entire house today too. Why not finish the rest while I do it. I can always run up to the liquor store; it's still early. Let's get to that stinking laundry. Where are my keys? I think I'm still feeling good enough to drive.

Okay, now that I'm back, I can really do some work. But first, a nice cocktail might help me ease into things. Wow, I guess I forgot to put these plates in the dishwasher yesterday. I'm certainly saving us on our electric bill.

I can't believe that my glass is already empty. It's happy

hour somewhere in the world; I might as well have another. The floors look like they haven't been washed in weeks. I'll add that to my itinerary. I certainly deserve another drink with this kind of agenda.

Maybe I should make a pot of coffee before I get started. I could use a real boost right about now. You know what? This place looks just fine as it is. I'm completely tired having to do all this housework anyway. I've done enough for today. I've surely earned the right to sit down and have a few more drinks.

Action

When I was drinking, I thought I was taking action to quit drinking. There inside the bottle all by myself, I prayed to the "do nothing" God with an earnest request that today would be the final day of utter inebriation. Tomorrow, I would behave myself. I did this over and over and over again. By the time I conceded to the reality that my body was truly defeated, I knew one thing for sure; my actions to resolve my compelling need to drink just didn't work. I never really acted on anything at all. I was merely performing in my made-up world.

Recovery doesn't allot time for wallowing in the resistance toward action, meditation, or prayer. I had to accept these principles in the most basic way. When relapse is on the horizon, prayer and action are monumental requirements to survive. Be on notice, there is a *big* difference between a want and a need. The alcoholic needs to take action and needs to find spirituality. Wanting anything at all is just desire without the maintenance.

I command myself every morning to pray to my Higher Power, who I call God. I spend at least thirty minutes in gratitude and meditation. And in all honesty, there are days when I just don't feel like doing it. Sometimes I am so busy that the thought of spending time with God interferes with my well planned schedule. But on those days when I opt out, I can clearly see my newly found serenity decrease. There is no doubt in my mind that my dedication to spirituality must take precedence.

I am compelled to do the necessary things to safeguard my sobriety even when I would rather lounge around. Attending meetings is a primary function in my daily living. They have become a stress-relieving injection when my mind wanders toward those devious thoughts of drinking again. I act on the wisdom of my sponsor when I need to hear a voice of support. I focus on creating sober friendships. I help another alcoholic whenever I can. I continually strive to maintain my recovery by doing whatever it takes.

The pursuit of spirituality and action are requirements. My true desire is to stop drinking, and if I am intent on reaching this goal, then I must supply my recovery with strength, hope, and constant dedication. Inaction always allows my disease the space to taunt me with all the reasons why I can have just one more drink. A single slipup for me only leads to serious consequences based solely on the evidence of my past.

Places I Don't Belong

My life has changed in recovery. I have come to accept, at least for the time being, that there are certain places where I don't belong right now. My purpose for today is to remain sober. Everything else ranks second

I certainly don't need to be running off to the bar just because my friends miss me at happy hour. It's not the best idea to hit that all-night party on New Year's Eve. Champagne toasts at midnight would be no match for me. Waking up without a thudding headache might be nice for a change. It's not the greatest plan to head into the liquor store for a pack of cigarettes. The gas station sells them too; it's probably a safer bet. There is absolutely nothing I need to buy in the wine aisle at the grocery store. It's smarter to push my cart toward the soda section.

Placing myself in front of those types of temptations just isn't worth it at this stage. I don't need to create needless triggers which could otherwise be avoided. There is simply no point in inviting danger when I don't have to.

I have chosen to avoid those places for now. Instead, I have decided to experience new activities. There is so much more to the world than spending grueling hours in the darkness of a bottle. Long walks with my dog, volunteer work, movies, coffee shops, service to others, new friendships, visits to new places, and so on guide my days in a happier direction. Life can be lived peacefully without alcohol.

I have had to open different doors while changing my course. Right now, I simply cannot return to parts of my previous road. I have no reason to arouse those luring attractions. I am safe where I am, in the arms of recovery. There is no other place more important than that.

Blame Game

I became really good at blaming everyone else for my problems. My intoxication always told me that if it wasn't for that certain situation or person, I surely wouldn't be in this predicament. I couldn't comprehend how other people were getting away with this position they had put me in. Their choices for me led to this result.

And there I would sit with a bottle in hand, whiling away the hours with a growing utter contempt toward everyone I loved. The more I drank, the more I saw my glaring troubles add up. My personal disappointments were always due to someone else's expectations of how I should live my life. Before the day was over, I had developed a long list of vindictive ways to get back at each of them for making me see myself under this bleak microscope.

Of course, in this mental state, I was always the victim. I was the martyr who dutifully followed the rules which had ruined my life. I began to see myself as the devoted subject who complacently obeyed the directives dealt out by society. I was convinced that my life had never been my own, and I could easily catalogue every controlling expectation which had ever been forced upon me. I was committed to the alcoholic lie that

I never had any opportunity to choose what I really wanted.

My insanity expanded each time I placed the blame on someone else for causing me to drink this way. I could name every dilemma they had triggered and initiated. I could go back to childhood tribulations which led me to this desire, to wallow in the bottle. My befuddled theories always resulted in finger-pointing. My life had gone this way because somebody else had made all the decisions. And I was mad as hell!

I thrived on the blame game...until I discovered rational thinking in sobriety. It was rather grueling to unveil the realities of all my past finger-pointing. It took strength to unearth the buried parts of my past, where the blame and the ultimate decision making had actually belonged to me. I realized that the vast majority of all the catalogued mistakes were mostly my own. I accepted the fact that nobody made me do anything I didn't say "yes" to.

In time, I was able to develop thick skin, facing each person and situation with a more solid frame of mind. I came to discern what really happened in every past decision I had made. I admitted that it was I who had played a role in those choices. This self-awareness inched my soul toward peace and understanding. I no longer needed to blame anyone for anything. There in the quiet solitude of acceptance, I finally released my bitter need to accuse others for the consequences of my own desire to drink.

The Party

I'm not going to lie; I need you to understand how much I struggled last night at the party. I was entirely focused on the fact that I was not drinking. I enviously watched everyone choose which cocktail they wanted, while I sipped on my glass of un-fulfilling sparkling water. Utter disappointment urged my brain to question this choice of recovery. The subject came up more than once. The truth is that I couldn't concentrate on anything else. The snickering temptation consumed me, and any previous goal to have a good, normal conversation was simply out of the question.

I'm not going to lie. My suffering wasn't a figment of my imagination. I could physically feel my desire to stay sober turn right toward defeat. The only flavor of the atmosphere was the intense odor of the alcohol permeating my senses. I wanted more, like a dog sniffing a scent. My invisible antennas spiked up, luring my thoughts into giving me permission to steal just one little drink. My eyes noticed the opened bottle only inches away. I can sufficiently tell you that my nervousness was absolute.

I am not going to lie. I hated every second of trying to paste on that glossy smile while the crowd around me chattered on with natural grins. Even in that big room, I felt utterly claustro-phobic and sincerely alone. I craved isolation and gratefully cowered in my own self-absorption. I sufficiently avoided most conversations by ignoring everyone. I simply couldn't ease into normal exchanges.

I am not going to lie. The race for my mental well-being was on, and I was being eaten alive by the intensity to survive this. But I had to keep my wits about me because I could see that you were having a little fun. You deserved a few hours of entertainment. So, I began counting how many drinks were being poured. I secretly tabulated who was drinking too much and who was already switching to coffee. I observed every detail with a desperate quest to ease my own nagging deliberations.

I am not going to lie. I reeled in contempt for every single person there. I was not, nor could I ever be, a normal drinker. I had to force myself to face this fact as I lingered in the security of the empty corner of the room. I felt a surge of anger so pervasive that I wanted to start lashing out all my pounding grievances to anyone who would listen. Instead, I quietly wallowed in self-pity. I was the outsider, the misfit, the alcoholic. No amount of laughter or high-spirited energy filling the room could alter my embattled emotions.

I am not going to lie. I really struggled last night at the party. The difficulties far outweighed the pleasures. The hours moved along like painful years. I was challenged in ways you can never fully understand. But I needed to confront these demons for both of us.

I am not going to lie. I wavered in my recovery at that party last night. I had to make minute-by-minute decisions which you will never have to make. But I clearly achieved a result only another alcoholic could fully comprehend; I didn't pick up that drink.

The Miracle of Living without It

"If I quit drinking, I'll never have the nerve to dance again." "It's a scary world out there: I'd hate to have to face it without a little sip." "I'm not quite sure how I might handle people; the bottle has always given me so much courage." "I already have a complicated life; the thought of tackling sobriety is too overwhelming." "I can't imagine going to bars and parties minus that cocktail in hand. I can't even fathom what the holiday season could be like without it." "No drinking equals no fun; I will certainly be left out with nothing to do." "One boring day, after another, that's how it will be." "Living life without alcohol just doesn't seem possible."

Here's the truth...Never in my wildest imagination did I believe that I could ever live without alcohol. The sheer idea of getting along in a world devoid of the bottle always made me pause. It was a huge part of my life; it was my lifeline in managing everything I did. So, the most remote possibility of removing it from my daily routine seemed daunting and unrealistic. But then, my life wasn't turning out too well with it, either.

Here's the truth...Alcohol was my tool to survive. I needed it to cope in order to feel anything at all. It was a complete part of me. Admitting that it was running my life into the ground would surely crush my chances of surviving in the real world. These harrowing debates with myself kept me drinking for a very long time, until I finally conceded that it was almost killing me.

Here's the truth...Living without alcohol can actually be done. The biggest surprise came when I realized that my life had become so much better without it. It was stunning to discover that I could get through emotions, events, and routines without being drunk. I could remember things from the day before and I clearly understood how I felt about them. I was able to experience the benefits of a healthy body and the contentment of having mental stability.

Here's the truth...It is possible. Life mysteriously works so much better without it when choosing to stick with sobriety. Recovery becomes a normal, happy way of living. The greatest epiphany of all came when I began wondering why I ever drank at all.

Defense Mechanisms

My irrational thoughts exploded when I dove into the bottle. I grew suspect to the whispered conversations by the people closest to me. Every inch of my being understood that their discussions always centered on my habit. I could sense their persistent irritations with me. I had to protect myself from their badgering insistence that I had a problem. The only way I could conquer these ongoing thoughts was to use defense mechanisms.

I justified my actions with unreasonable logic. I tried to use my "smarts" by explaining matters away. I minimized my drunken mistakes by avoiding the subject. I tried to make miraculous recoveries by following new rules my family insisted on. After a few long days of obedience, I quietly crept back to what I really wanted to do. I was proficiently brilliant at denying my part in some bad scenario, which I had actually caused.

I figured out how to blame other people for my volatile behavior. I easily convinced myself that these continual messy situations were never my fault. I discovered that my derogatory sarcasm could definitely stave off some arguments. I projected my own concerns about my drinking by mocking other people who also drank a bit too much. I often played stupid by acting like I didn't understand the issue. I learned to redirect a conversation if it somehow pointed in my direction.

I fought hard at manipulating my family by staying clean for as long as I could. I played the victim card when I knew that my friends seemed nervous about my excessive drinking. I operated with the primary intent of making those around me focus on someone else other than me. I knew when to derail a topic which ultimately might lead to a discussion about alcohol.

I managed to alter real-life problems by rearranging the truth. I sometimes succeeded in creating sweet atonements, which might allow me the freedom to keep drinking. Once in a while I acted with a negative slant, forcing others to stay away from me. I used and abused those I truly loved with a menacing defense and an irrational determination to devote myself to the bottle.

Revisiting the Past

Every so often, when that devil is on my shoulder uttering a few lies about how it's time once again to have a few drinks, I have to revisit the dark mistakes of my past. The unsightliness of these memories is always enough to help me jump that momentary hurdle. In an instant, I can recall the gray fog enveloping my body. I can envision myself passed out on the couch after hours of intense inebriation. I watch how I finally rise and stumble toward the coffeemaker. I hear my slurred speech while talking to someone on the phone. My physical capabilities are slow and dragged. I am utterly impaired.

I listen to my own empty weeping in the shower. I see myself start arguments for the sake of defending my obvious intoxication. I notice the places where I have slyly hidden my bottles. I hear myself retching in the nearest bathroom. I sadly observe my family looking at me in total despair.

I spot my hands trembling as I am trying to reach for more water. The bed is unmade again and the dishes are smelling funny in the sink. I conclude that I am sitting on the floor, because I am trying to remember what happened yesterday. My bedroom reeks of silent destitution, and my body is quivering with the pangs of shame.

I detect that my mind had already succumbed to the world of the wasted. I see myself swallow just one more drink in order to forget what I am doing. I hear my brain churning, already formulating new lies about my day. I notice my family hiding in their safe corners so that they don't have to see me like this. I witness the effects of my own loneliness and confinement. I see that I am nearing the end.

The distant, dark places in my past remind me of what will happen if I swallow just one drink. These disturbing recollections reignite my desire to remain sober. They mercifully invoke that absolute reason why I must never live like that again. One memory can cure that one moment when alcohol seems to be the only answer.

Morning Drink
Alarm Bell

"Am I really going to do this? No, I'll just go downstairs and make some coffee, drink some water, and sit down for a minute." "Well, that didn't work. I've got to stop this shaking somehow." "Absolutely not; I am not going to have a drink this early in the morning, which would be utter insanity for sure." "God, I am really feeling awful." "Okay just stop for a second and drink some more water. Go ahead, keep it down."

"Maybe in a little while, I'll take a drink." "Surely it has to be closer to noon by now." "I must be crazy; I've only been up for less than hour. Now what am I going to do?" "All right, let's get one thing straight right now; I am *not* an alcoholic." "One tiny pick-me-up this morning won't hurt." "I promise that I'll never do this again. It's just this once." "Boy, that helped; I'm feeling like a million dollars already!"

I wildly talked to myself like that before succumbing to the morning drink. I grappled with that decision from there on in. I knew that my alcohol problem was fiercely raging forward once I fell headfirst into my early-morning excuse for intoxication. The impish inner voice justified my need for it. My body often revolted from that choice when I immediately scrambled to the bathroom to vomit. Yet, even on those more sickly days, I ran right back to the bottle as soon as I could.

Somewhere in the recesses of my mind, an alarm bell was loudly going off. Its boisterous ringing sounded continuous warnings that I was in serious trouble. I could hear them clearly, and I knew that a real madness had overtaken me. The morning requirement pursued me, and I excused it, allowing the depths of my alcoholism to swell into full-blown insanity.

Thoughts of My Alcoholic Friend

I am thinking of you today, my friend. I know you are still out there, clinging to all the lies the bottle once spoke to me. I know you are suffering. I know that you are probably getting tired of your anguished routine. I know you are alone and broken. Even now, in my own serenity-centered sobriety, I can feel your pain from a distance.

I am praying for you today, my friend. I am appealing to my God, to make His way toward you. I understand your reasons to remain in the darkness. I was once hiding there myself. I can hear your silent pleas for help. You lay awake long into the night, terrified about who you have become. I have dreamed your same nightmares.

I am wondering about you today, my friend. Are you sick again? Did you try to tell yourself it was the flu? Or have you reached for that morning drink to solve the problem? I remember how much it initially helped me. Right now, you are probably telling yourself that there is no shame in it. This type of medicinal use is the same as aspirin, right? It's the best way to justify the need. I too once used all those excuses.

I am speculating about you today, my friend. I sense your

despondency this very second. You keep trying to climb out of the hole but end up falling back in. Your body is aching, your head is throbbing, and you are so very scared. I know; mine hurt in much the same way, and it terrified me to the very core.

I am reflecting on you today, my friend. I am fully aware of your continued guilt and outright disgrace. You are humiliated by your blackout last night. Your confusion is encompassing your life. You know now that others are concerned for your welfare. This awareness stirs up a trembling fear. I remember those heavy moments myself.

I am reaching for you today, my friend. I want you to put out your hand as I once did long ago. Go ahead, feel my touch. I know and understand how hard this is. I had to find the courage as well. It's going to be all right; freedom is just around the corner. I come without judgment. I too was once where you are now. I beckon you to follow me to safety and hope.

I promise to you today, my friend, that I will stand by you, for I sat in your place of pride and humiliation. I vow to you today, my friend, that you are not alone in your illness. I beg of you today, my friend, to let go of your worries. Walk into the light and be with me. Surrender today, my friend. This choice will take you to a renewed life filled with serenity and joy. It's okay now, my friend. Your anxiety will pass soon. Mine did as well when I chose to take the hand of another alcoholic.

Grateful

I am grateful for my sobriety today. The small miracles of daily living continue to blossom. I am thankful that I am no longer alone. I am developing courage while letting go of fear. The morning sunshine is a welcome. The dark days are behind me. I am embracing the world with energy. I have chosen to become a part of it once more.

I am grateful for my sobriety today. I have been graced with a second chance. I am no longer withered away by the antagonizing lure of the bottle. I am pursuing radiant opportunities with abounding hope. I have chosen to stand clear of isolation and negativity. I am worthy of self-respect.

I am grateful for my sobriety today. Within it, I have renewed my spirit with dignity and honor. The essence of those qualities have given me fortitude to carry on. I am capable of doing things I never thought I could do. I have gained confidence and conviction once more. I have come to understand that drinking only dissolves this joyous momentum. I am entitled to smile about these incredible achievements.

I am grateful for my sobriety today. Without it, I would be confined to the reckless echoes of insanity. I am present, I am a person, and I am living in reality. I have been blessed by opting for this freedom. I am doing just fine at this moment. I am thankful for the here and now, and that's all I need today.

Shame

I couldn't have been any more ashamed of myself! Any slight pursuit of decency when I was drinking was inevitably demolished. All my early presumptions of who I would be someday were completely erased. There was nothing left of my being except a ghastly figure who was entirely absorbed in a bottle filled with guilt. I detested every ounce of who I had become. I wanted to die.

This utter disgust could be formidably forgotten when I drank. Alcohol was like a bandage, covering up the oozing scars beneath. It helped me to see the lighter side of the monstrous personality spewing out before my very eyes. I was caught up in a vicious cycle of wanting to get better and opting to ignore my complete degradation.

The more I ran with the bottle, the more disgrace I would bring to my shame. The more shame I accrued, the more I needed to get rid of it. When I opted to stay sober for a single day, the images of all the chaos I had created consumed me. A couple of hours of this wasn't worth the reality of who I had become.

I could not find mercy anywhere. A moment of comfort could no longer be attained. The pain of embarrassment, humiliation, and sorrow pursued my every move. I was thoroughly entrapped by insistent nagging and discouraging judgments of myself. These contemptuous voices were not imagined, and they recklessly echoed inside my mind.

Sobriety has led me to a comfortable place where I have been released from that incessant shame. I have been able to face those demons which once ravaged my mind. I am no longer smothered by my past. I am a step ahead of the negative influences only alcohol could bring. I can freely feel the joy of no longer having to be ashamed.

I'm Sorry

I am so very sorry for all the pain I have caused you. I finally understand how much I hurt you. I wish that I could take it all back. I wish I could change everything. I never intended to do this much damage. I brutally realize that my actions directly affected every part of you. I sincerely never wanted this to happen.

I am so very sorry for choosing the bottle over your loving relationship. It didn't occur to me that I was pushing you away. I wish that I could rewind everything. I regret that I made you worry every hour of the day. I know that I never took the time to notice your look of exhaustion. I realize that my desire to drink replaced my desire to stay true to you.

I am so very sorry for assuming that your only role was to take care of me. I was consumed by alcohol, and your wishes meant nothing. I am ashamed that I lacked sensitivity and decency during that time. I didn't mean to be that selfish. I never thought that my isolation was producing so much chaos.

I am very sorry for all the embarrassment I have caused you during these terribly long years. You did not deserve that constant humiliation. I apologize for all the times you had to swallow your pride in order to defend me. I yearn to erase those harrowing moments. I redden with shame when I recall how you mustered the strength to clean up my mess yet again. I understand now how intolerable I was.

I am very sorry for how my disease battered your pursuit to live happily. I was a contaminated human being whose only quest was to exist without you. With deep remorse, I know today that I injured you profoundly. I am truly sorry for everything in the past which left us broken. I wish the memories could be altered and the sadness erased. I make this amend with an honest commitment to change and repair. Whether you can forgive me is up to you. I only know that I truly never meant to cause this much pain.

Notorious Quotations

"You're really not listening, you're really not!" "Leave me alone right now; I have a lot on my plate." "Stop nagging me about the way I do things." "Can't this conversation wait until tomorrow?" "I've heard enough of your put-downs for one day." "Is anything ever enough for you?" "You certainly have a way of always making me feel bad." "Right now is *not* the time to discuss this."

"Go ahead, keep ignoring me." "Forget I just said that." "I've had a bad day, so don't bother me with silly questions." "I told you a thousand times that I hate going out with those people." "I think I have earned the right to take a nap." "Could you possibly tone your voice down?" "Yep, you know it all." "Of course you noticed that I forgot to do one little thing."

"I am sick and tired of all your petty reminders." "You know what? You don't get it."

"Good, I didn't want to be there with you anyway." "That's right, you do everything around here." "And you think *I'm* the crazy one." "It's impossible to get a word in edgewise." "I'm certainly entitled to miss a family outing for a change." "Please stop screaming; I'm standing directly in front of you."

"You're the one playing games." "Can we ever enjoy a

moment of peace around here?" "Do we have to argue about everything?" "I just know that I didn't say it like that." "You're right, I'm wrong; let's leave it at that." "I can't take much more of your finger-pointing." "Wow, you've got some nerve to talk to me like that! I think it's a good idea if you go in the other room."

"Enough said, I get the picture." "I'm guessing that you just love to irritate the hell out of me." "I knew you would disregard my suggestion." "You're the one who creates negativity in this house." "Believe me, I've heard you say that a million times." "Is there any chance you could get off my back?" "I don't need to say I'm sorry." "You totally stress me out." "I told you that I would get to it tomorrow. Why are you freaking out again?"

"I am not overdrinking." "I wasn't the one who finished the bottle." "I did not pass out last night." "I remember everything." "You are overanalyzing me." "You went right along with me." "I'm adult enough to know when to stop." "Are you watching over me again?" "I don't need any more of your humiliation." "Please help me; I'm in trouble."

Recovery Is a Lifestyle

Recovery is a lifestyle. There are continual changes I'm making each day. The switch from being an inebriated human being to a sober one sometimes feels extreme. My universe has spun into a 180-degree transformation in only a short time. The presence of today is completely different from how I operated yesterday.

I have had to alter most areas in my life. I have maintained some of my old friendships, but I have had to moderate others. I have learned to be firm when saying no to something which might harm my sobriety. I have dealt with the fact that I cannot always commit to a party if I'm feeling vulnerable. I have come to accept that certain events will go on without me. I stave off that urge to swim in self-pity when this happens.

I have restored relationships which I once thought could never be repaired. I have managed to create sober friendships along the way. I have delighted in certain activities which I once believed were completely dull. I have challenged myself in endeavors that seemed useless before.

I have pursued my talents with a vigorous effort. I have come to seek wellness in my body and soul. I have learned to occupy my time with rewarding results. I have allowed my heart to embrace the true definition of happiness, something I hadn't felt in years.

Recovery is a revolution of the spirit. It is a deft-defying change filled with a new set of standards. Recovery is a daily resolve to live without alcohol. It is a lifestyle filled with the pleasures of freedom and serenity, which I am willing to work for. It is a faithful companion when I wake up each morning, and a tranquil presence when I go to bed each night.

The Bad Stories

If you think that your story is bad, you should hear mine. It seemed every alcoholic in the room had a noteworthy, harrowing tale to tell. Under the influence of this destructive disease, lives had fallen apart in different ways.

Many people had encountered situations with the law. DUIs seemed to pile up in most of the narratives. Blackouts had led to all sorts of misbehavior; disorderly conduct, various misdemeanors, felonies, or total memory loss regarding a series of events were common. Some of us did time in a jail cell or institution. Divorce prevailed with brutal force. Oftentimes, the loss of children ensued in a custody battle.

There are those who lost teeth due to falls. A few were already succumbing to liver and kidney diseases. Broken arms, severe bruises, and other health-related problems were not uncommon. Suicide and death-related car accidents weren't issues that could be passed over.

Some people luckily managed to avoid those things. But their lives had grown unmanageable in other ways. Lost jobs, unemployment, homelessness, and sometimes bankruptcy ran the gambit. Doctors, lawyers, teachers, and other professionals were no longer deemed responsible enough to maintain their careers. State licensing and various certifications were often revoked. Many of these once highly skilled individuals were now looking for any type of work

Friendships had been broken. Themes of loneliness and isolation prevailed. People sadly portrayed an accounting of spoiled holidays when the corruption of alcohol ruined the season. Some elderly folks miserably admitted that they were no longer welcomed to visit their grandchildren.

In the life of every alcoholic, a loss could be reported and a deep sadness conveyed. It didn't matter where you lived, who you were, or how much money was in your pocket; the disease had destroyed someone or something in your life.

I am ever mindful of all the inevitable consequences equated with alcoholism. I am fully aware of the debilitating roads it leads us to. Today I choose recovery, because the reality of choosing to drink will only take me to problematic places where suffering abounds and losses accrue.

Turning Over My Will

There were no other options left. I had to turn my will and my life over to the care of the God of my understanding. Your God might be different than mine, and my prayers different from yours. I find value in my religion, while you may not see it that way. We are all made up of different opinions and varied belief systems. Even so, every alcoholic will tell you that eventually they turned their problems over to their God, no matter what or who they named. Somewhere along the way, they had to choose a new ruler to oversee their lives.

I often like to describe this decision like this...When I was running the show, I couldn't manage anything. When I was making decisions with the bottle by my side, I was only creating a bigger mess in my life. When I was the Higher Power, I caused havoc, chaos, and total destruction for myself and those I loved. When I was in charge, happiness and freedom did not reign. My kingdom was overgrown with turmoil, and I had inadvertently deserted the throne.

The only possible way to any reasonable solution was to ultimately make the decision to allow my God to take my place instead. The utter upheaval of my past efforts as a leader warranted it. I was certainly not a success, and the shattered pieces of my life proved it. I absolutely had to accept that I could no longer live under my own power.

I accepted defeat and took the hand of my God. I surrendered to the obvious fact that I needed guidance and direction from someone other than myself. Somehow, once I let go of my desire to run my own show, a wave of tranquility materialized. I could breathe soundly, knowing that my life was handed over to the care of my God. This release of control gave me the permission to follow a new lead, to grasp a new concept, and to clear the way toward a true sober beginning.

Choosing Isolation

Alcoholism breeds loneliness and isolation. Your secret is only safe with you. It is a silent, aching burden which eats away at your very soul. You are aware of your own deterioration. You are mystified with your resolve to let it continue. You are in constant fear of your need to keep drinking.

You tell yourself that nobody could ever comprehend why you are compelled to drain yourself with these worries, day in and day out. Far worse, they could never fathom why it is that you seemingly drink without pause. Your personal terror insidiously grows stronger with each passing hour. You desperately want to share your distress, but you believe that no one would ever understand. Your secret is far too dark in nature.

You are alone in your insanity. You push everyone away because you have become a psychotic, opting not to frighten them with your thoughts. It is far easier to isolate and figure out this problem on your own. You have grown certain that this kind of horror has never happened to anyone else. The best way to handle such madness is to hide from the rest of the world. A secret of this magnitude is far too heavy to be revealed.

Your nagging discomfort increases as you watch other people living normally, when you know you are not. Your mind is erupting with anxiety, but you dare not expose these concerns. You have abandoned life because of this searing problem. There is nothing left for you to do but stay clear of people as much as you can. This solitary choice keeps your secret secure.

You exist with this loneliness to preserve your own safety. You willingly sanction the absolute madness. You covet your solitude because you have freely chosen to abandon reality. The stinging truths about your life are far too horrific to be shared. It's the easiest way to protect your loved ones from this menacing secret.

Pleasantries of Normal Living

I am surprised when I hear actual laughter boom from within. It's a pleasant feeling to have a conversation which honestly makes sense. Reading a good book or watching a movie is completely relaxing. I thoroughly enjoy glasses of sparkling water or soda without hesitation. I'm astounded at my ability to be in rhythm with daily routines.

I'm in awe of a good night's rest. I'm grateful for my thoughtful morning prayers. I'm comfortable with my clear opinion on certain matters. It's nice to be abreast of worldly news events. I'm impressed by my capability to gracefully express my disappointments. I like the fact that I am no longer that disruptive person in the room.

I enjoy a body which can finish a long walk. It's pleasant to hear my voice speaking cohesively for a change. I'm grateful that I possess sound reasoning when I'm dealing with problems. I enjoy the essence of resourcefulness when I need to complete a long day. I appreciate quiet evenings of accomplishments.

I relish the delicious taste of food. I'm happy with my ever-evolving personality. I look forward to tomorrow. I applaud my willingness to jump hurdles, even if the achievement is something that almost anyone could attain. I take pride in the strength I have when facing the challenges of sobriety. I don't mind rewarding myself with ice cream if I've had a difficult day.

I breathe much easier knowing that people have chosen to be with me. I'm experiencing the happiness of being loved. I feel the pulse of loving again. I'm moved by compliments. I'm aware of the strides I'm making. I relish in the freedom of my creativity. I'm excited to share the events of my day.

I'm grateful for every inch of my recovery, for it has opened the door to the pleasures of normal living. I'm learning and growing because of it. I'm slowly finding my sense of being. Each new day brings discovery and blessings, which I had never had the opportunity to realize at the bottom of the bottle.

I Couldn't Be an Alcoholic

I couldn't possibly be an alcoholic. I mean, seriously, so what if I drink every day? Who cares if I can guzzle a cocktail quicker than the rest of the gang? It's no big news flash that my body tolerates an extreme amount of liquor for my size; I've been doing it for years. Sure, my friends seem to get a little annoyed when I order too many rounds. It's my way of enjoying those festive moments together. So if I missed a few days of work, what's the problem? I have a bunch of sick days coming to me anyway.

Okay, so I was late on a few payments. Credit card companies are notorious for changing due dates. My family has forced me to see that counselor again. I don't mind. An hour a week is worth keeping them happy. DUIs are a dime a dozen; they're the modern-day tickets. Mine just became another statistic.

Well, I can't help it if alcohol hits me the wrong way sometimes. I know for a fact that tolerance is different for everyone. Are you telling me that I had slurred speech again last night? How many times do I have to tell you that I'm on a diet? The cashiers at the liquor store know me by name. I chalk it off as my being one of the friendlier types.

You know how it is. Nothing seems to last in this house for very long. The only reason I hide bottles is because someone else around here continues to finish off the ones in the cabinet. I'm not much of a beer drinker, but I like to have it around, just in case. Last night is a bit of a blur. Everyone does a little forgetting at my age. Just asking is all...Will they be serving adult beverages tomorrow night? God knows that parties just aren't as much fun without it.

I'm totally fine with drinking alone. Some of the most notorious people created great works of art this way. Are you really telling me that I'm always worried about alcohol? Get one thing straight right now; tonight, I'm only drinking coffee. I couldn't possibly be an alcoholic.

Everyone else is drinking exactly the same way. Unlike me, they choose not to own up to it. *They* are the ones with the problem.

Maintaining Sobriety

The mental work of maintaining sobriety can be difficult sometimes. There are days when I just don't feel like cranking up the effort to pray to my Higher Power or plan out my day with a willing focus. Once in a while, I'm not in the mood to surrender to the realities of my disease. Every so often, I simply want to be lazy, relax on the couch, and inevitably miss a meeting. There are moments when I tire of my daily rituals necessary to achieve continued recovery.

Life happens, and this kind of weariness occurs. Routines frustrate everyone sometimes, even the people who are not battling addiction. The truth is that while we were drinking, schedules and "to-do" lists weren't habits. Our only agenda item was to find a way to become thoroughly intoxicated. This was our foremost priority. We were minimalists, only set on accomplishing what was absolutely necessary in order to drink. Pestering commitments were cleverly set aside.

So we were used to that kind of thinking. Then, we quit drinking and joined the world, whereby people actually follow general rules each day. The whole process of living becomes new to us. It's almost like learning to walk all over again. We take one step, and then another. We learn to fall and get back up. We slowly become stable when we follow this direction. We surrender to the structure of truly becoming a breathing, active human being once more.

Effort is part of the ritual. Will is a piece of the process. Accepting our illness is a daily responsibility. Prayer, meditation, and hard work should always be factored into our daily routines. Life happens, and we must face it openly. Sobriety remains when we choose to honor the choices available to us. Laziness only breeds mindless contemplation, which opens the door to vulnerability and possible relapse.

I Was Never Brought Up to Lie

"I did pay those bills several days ago. In fact, I'm looking at them still in front of me." "Of course I set up the dog's vet appointment. I'd better find that number for the office." "I'm sorry, but I had to call in sick yesterday. It was that twenty-four-hour flu again." "I probably shouldn't have had that last glass of wine." "Don't worry, the bar tab was pretty reasonable." "Jeez, did I really leave a twenty-dollar tip?" "Yes, I told you already that I mailed it in." "I have no idea what she's talking about. I did not make a fool of myself last night." "If only I could remember what I did."

I was never brought up to lie. As a matter of fact, I was never good at it until the overwhelming need to drink surpassed the need to be truthful. What mattered most was staying ahead of the constant questioning, and the only possible way to do this was to be dishonest about almost everything in my life.

I didn't want this, nor did I enjoy concocting these tall tales. But I knew that everyone was watching me; I had to look normal and reasonable. I felt as if I had no other choice. I recognized that I was fooling myself. Yet, the alcohol pardoned this by making me believe that little white lies never hurt anyone.

As time went on, my entire life seemed to be built on half-truths, most of which I could no longer recall. My world got messy with fabricated clutter. I couldn't catch up, nor could I risk examining the actual facts. The fear of what I might find there was unsettling. Alcohol had definitely made a liar out of me. Its possession erased my moral character, principled lifestyle, and sense of integrity. It cleverly created a person I was never brought up to be.

The Stigma of Alcoholism

I had to come to terms with the fact that many people do not grasp the disease of alcoholism. There are plenty of folks who unwittingly point fingers at us with self-righteous convictions. We can be called drunks, bums, addicts, and losers. We are often considered to be immoral, unprincipled, senseless human beings. We might be told that we have no willpower, fortitude, or strength of character. Some may say that we are just plain stupid for drinking too much. And still others may refuse to understand why it is that we can't stop.

Some doctors, nurses, and even mental health professionals reject the fact that alcoholism is a disease. Unfortunately, there are still judges, parole officers, and other disciplinarian types who rebuff the proven facts of addiction. Many of us land in jail or psych wards because of it.

Even in the modern age, we alcoholics fear the gossip and misnomers of our disease. Sometimes, we are hesitant to admit our alcoholism because of these unfair labels. Many of us choose isolation for fear of ridicule. We can be desperately afraid of rumors derived from the term *alcoholic*. Tragedy has come for many of us because of this misunderstanding.

I knew all this and felt all these noted fears when I drank. I was hiding my problem for a reason, and yet, I didn't really understand it all that well myself. I despised being a drunk, and the type of loser who did not have the strength to beat the bottle. Something was desperately wrong with me, but the notion of being titled an "alcoholic" seemed daunting. This kind of category conveyed dereliction and failure.

My illness will probably never be as reasonably understood as other diseases might. Cancer, diabetes, and most physical maladies were researched, succinctly categorized, and medically defined. Individuals with those such troubles weren't running around causing chaos, slurring their words, and driving off to buy more alcohol than they needed. Addiction was simply harder to make sense of; it didn't come with an exact format. It mixed a physical allergy with a mental outcome, which was often different for everyone.

Once in recovery, I learned the concrete facts as to why I incessantly drank. I know now that all the misrepresented interpretations of my disease are false. I am an alcoholic whose brain cannot process alcohol like other people. One drink leads to another, which leads to full-fledged chaos when I do. The only way to combat my illness is to stop drinking. This lone solution allows me to accept the steps of recovery.

I may not always be understood by those who choose to view alcoholism as a character defect. I may never be able to convince them otherwise. What actually matters is that I know what I suffer from. The only life I can truly manage is my own. What other people prefer to describe me as is their own problem. My only focus for today is my personal sobriety and wellness.

Accepting Help

One of my many faults is that I run my life on self-will. I am just the type who considers the term *help* a defect in itself. I definitely have this tendency to want to do everything my own way. This self-bravado and obstinate determination has not exactly led to the best results in my life. Somewhere along the way, I concluded that asking for help equates to weakness.

The fact that I used to like bucking the system hurled me into a boatload of consequences. My own fixes for my progressing drinking problem certainly weren't working. And every time I thought I discovered the cure, I'd find that bottle back in my hands quicker than I intended.

As a recovering alcoholic, I had to quickly figure out that I needed help. I couldn't just "do it on my own," and the chances of remaining sober by my individualized willpower was not going to work. I needed to surrender my obstinate, stubborn soul to a Higher Power; I needed the fellowship of other alcoholics, and I needed a sponsor.

I was admittedly desperate enough to develop a relationship with my God. Conceding and welcoming spirituality made me feel as if I was being counseled by a protective force who deemed me worth saving. I liked the freedom of this paired relationship. This positive step seemed to grant me a sense of peace. I wasn't alone anymore.

But while my God was guarding my recovery and listening to my prayers, I was still a human being walking the earth with daily challenges. God didn't talk back and He wasn't driving me to meetings.

I needed conversations with other people who understood my challenges. I had to recognize that sobriety demanded more than just myself. It was completely impossible to "go it alone." This was a bitter pill for me to swallow because self-sufficiency had been my motto for many years. Support was a necessity if I was truly planning to recover.

I took the step forward, earnestly praying for the right sponsor. In a short time, I found one who suited me perfectly. I learned that all alcoholics run on self-will and that I was not unaccompanied in this trait. I slowly accepted the help of other alcoholics, family, and friends. I eventually let go of that far-fetched idea that my struggle was only mine to deal with. I have come to realize that asking for help does not signify weakness; rather, it gives me strength and a unified courage to pursue a sober life.

Vacation

"A beach vacation? Are you kidding me? I guess I'm supposed to watch everyone else drink those luscious-colored cocktails while I glare with desire." "God knows that minibar in my room will be beckoning me." "I'm going to end up just sitting there with elaborate daydreams about how I might simply try just one." "I'll effortlessly recall all those times I had a buzz going by noon." "Bored, that's what I'll be. I'm not going to have any fun, that's for sure." "I can't believe that I'm even going to attempt this."

The thought of going on a sober vacation unnerved me. What was I going to do without alcohol? Jaunts away from home used to mean that I didn't need an excuse to drink. Everyone else was doing it too. I was easily caught up in the escape, and no one really noticed my intake. Vacations were the perfect time to look like a normal drinker.

Now my world had definitely changed. I wasn't sure how to take this kind of trip, absent of alcohol. Everything I had done before circled around it. I simply couldn't see how it could possibly be any fun. Although I knew that I might endure some difficult stretches, I also knew that my new life depended on attempting it. Vacations were normal events. I had to muster the courage to give it a try.

Admittedly, there were some difficult moments. There were instances when I had to take deep breaths. But for the first time in my life, I suddenly realized that there were many things I'd missed out on. "Water is meant for swimming." "Sand feels warm on your feet." "Morning sunshine is a beautiful sight." "Books are actually read in lounge chairs." "People are interesting to meet." "Pools are refreshing." "Food is worth tasting." "Walking along the beach is invigorating." "Activities are worthy of pleasure." "Touring is educational and interesting." "Restaurants do serve delicious nonalcoholic drinks." Memories are actually made and remembered.

I took the chance and took the trip where I encountered a new way of enjoying myself and others. I was renewed by the rest and the ultimate conclusion that I could actually have fun without drinking. I had jumped another hurdle in recovery, all the while discovering new and amazing things to do on a vacation.

I Am Safe Again Today

I'm safe again today. I know what I did yesterday. I'm pleasantly surprised that there's not one part of it I have forgotten. I'm thrilled to announce that I willingly flowed through the hours without pondering what time I would drink. I reveled in the excitement that I had far better plans.

I'm safe again today. My work has been accomplished cohesively; I have not left one item for tomorrow's to-do list. I was efficient, productive, and energetic. I will hit my pillow, knowing that I have performed to the best of my ability. I will sleep soundly in confidence and pride.

I'm safe again today. I happened to make a few mistakes along the way, but I fully took responsibility for them. I was friendly and kind to everyone. I'm truly enthused to have made so many new friends. I liked that my car drove right past the liquor store without stopping. I smiled with confidence once I hit the driveway.

I'm safe again today. My family was eager to have breakfast with me. I didn't sleep in, nor did I decline eating. I was part of the group and happily conversing. I'm finally enjoying the daylight hours without a thudding headache. I can't wait to get home for dinner.

I'm safe again today. I strolled through the neighborhood without a thought of being recognized as the one who smelled like liquor. I walked along the sidewalk feeling unfamiliar pangs of normalcy. I reveled in the sensation of belonging to humanity.

I'm safe again today. I'm present now in the land of the living. I'm reaping so many rewards. I'm grateful to have chosen recovery which allows me to be part of the simple pleasures of everyday life.

Dealing with Events

Well, this is just great. The family picnic is this weekend, and I'm expected to be there. Nobody knows that I'm in recovery. No doubt Uncle Jack is going to show up with coolers of beer. He's certainly going to crack one wide open as soon as he can. Am I *seriously* supposed to sit there and watch this? I'm probably going to have to spend all my time with Aunt Mary; she loves lemonade and knitting. It's going to be one long afternoon.

Christmas is going to be a real struggle. My cousins will be pouring the wine like its water. They love discussing the different fruity tastes, and that's all I'm going to hear. It will surely be the topic of conversation most of the time. So what am I going to say when they hand me a wineglass? Maybe I'll tell them that I'm sticking to vodka and soda and secretly pour some sparkling water instead. At least I'll look like I'm drinking.

Another party tomorrow night with the neighbors. That keg of beer is going to be glaring at me from their garage. I can already see myself wanting to slip in there when no one is looking. It's going to be a real issue as the night progresses when everyone starts getting that buzz. I'm going to have to do the practical thing and slyly creep home without notice.

A late-night dinner with the boss again on Tuesday. Two weeks ago, he drank three martinis before he finished his steak. It wasn't easy following his conversation after that, not to mention the fact that I was secretly salivating every time he took a sip. He wasn't too pleased when I ordered a Coke. I used the "I'm taking medication" fib which seemed to work. What am I going to tell him this time?

The summer festival starts this Friday. We have always gone in droves with our friends. The beer stand was usually our gathering place. Now what am I supposed to do? It's probably best to bring some extra money so that I can run off to play a few silly games. They'll be too busy drinking to realize that I've slunk away.

Adjusting to old events with new direction takes perseverance and discipline. There are a million ways to stay on track without drinking. Developing a standby plan is the best way to handle previous drinking affairs without alcohol. Most of the time, no one even notices that I have changed my direction, and I'm usually surprised on how good it all worked in the end.

The Mirror

I didn't always look like this. No, back then, my appearance was rarely my foremost concern. I minimally kept myself together in order to get by. What mattered more than anything was getting to that drink. Forcing myself to look presentable took far too much energy and work.

Once in a while I'd glance in the mirror just to check on myself. The bloated vision staring back at me sent shockwaves through my soul. It was obvious that alcohol was eating away at my appearance, and it concerned me. I didn't know how to cope with this bewildering evidence. The only practical solution was to avoid this problem by drinking some more.

As my buzzing mind progressed toward a desired state of bliss, I'd bravely look in the mirror a second time. The change had been all that I'd hoped for. The blotches, jaundiced eyes, and puckered skin had all been erased. Alcohol magically allowed my senses to perceive a healthy specimen. This sense of relief proved that I was acceptable again.

Each day I created a new version of myself. I erased blemishes and courageously crafted a perfect likeness of who I wanted to be. The trick was to remain drunk. Any other option taunted me with cold hard facts meant to expose the true nature of my physical appearance.

When I finally chose sobriety, the mirror was not initially my friend. A damaged, bloodied soul stood before me. I did not recognize myself at all. That glowing, healthy human being I had concocted before was certainly not staring in my direction. I was actually witnessing the destructive effects of alcoholism.

Today, the mirror has become my friend. Each morning I gaze at my fresh, renewed face and whitened eyes. My hair is combed; my teeth are brushed. There are no longer puffy edges around my cheeks. My reflection smiles with a healthy joy. Sobriety has helped me renew my physical appearance, which, in turn, provides me the joyful essence of normal living.

I Will Never Be a Normal Drinker

It gets hard sometimes. Out of the blue, a drink just sounds like a good idea, and I'm not talking about some kind of sweet soda. Usually when I have this sort of craving, I melt into self-pity. I get angry at other people who have the ability to make that choice. A bitter moment arises because I realize that I will never be a normal drinker. My past looks me straight in the eyes with the truth.

It gets hard sometimes. That little devil on my shoulder tends to whisper all the ways I could get around this sobriety thing. He likes to remind me that no one will find out if I have just one. But, I have been with this mischief maker before; he's a real pal at the beginning…until it comes time to break my fall.

It gets hard sometimes. Alcohol is pretty hard to avoid. It likes to glare at me at restaurants, bowling alleys, parties, festivals, barbeques, holiday gatherings, graduations, family dinners, and grocery stores. If I glare back long enough, I completely begin to focus on exactly the one thing I cannot have.

It gets hard sometimes. Sobriety is an amazing grace, but there are times when I feel irritable because of it. My life transformation is a process, a day-to-day commitment toward the crucial habits of recovery. I have come to accept this unequivocally. I am not a normal drinker who can choose between drinking a soda or drinking a beer. Bottles don't stare at these people, nor do devils taunt them with the whisper of a sip. They are not like me, and I am not like them. Surrendering to this concept is a necessity. I must grasp and concede to this new way of life. I will never be able to drink like they do. More importantly, I can never drink at all.

Declining a Drink

There are moments when I feel a bit self-conscious when declining a drink. I have been in awkward situations plenty of times. Those who know that I am an alcoholic tend to protectively hover over me. Sometimes this obvious attention makes me feel like a child. Servers, hosts, partygoers, acquaintances, and even distant friends who are not aware of my circumstances look at me quizzically when I choose a soda. In the beginning, I was quite uncomfortable.

Nervousness reigns, and I can't help but feel like the noticeable outsider during these events. My mind begins to chatter, convincing me that everyone knows who I really am. I wonder if they can see that "Scarlet A" for alcoholic stamped on my forehead. I have even sat quietly, trying to listen for all the gossip pertaining to my nonalcoholic cocktail. My disease likes to use this nice little trap by urging me to think that I am not like everyone else.

The real problem is twofold. First, even though I'd like to believe that everyone is noticing, most of them are not entirely interested in just me. Second, I am an alcoholic, and I am aware that one alcoholic beverage will only lead me to twenty more. This lone fact proves that my life depends on having to say "no." Normal drinking is not something I can do.

If I feel the need to save face for whatever reason, there are plenty of ways to go about doing it. Little white lies, or made-up excuses seem to do the trick. "Sorry, I'm on some heavy medication right now." "Not tonight, I'm really trying to lose weight." "I'm not in the mood; maybe later." "I've got to be up early in the morning, so I'm going to stick with water." "Lately, alcohol has been upsetting my stomach." "Truth be told, I'm on the wagon." This kind of necessary fibbing isn't wrong; it simply keeps me safe.

When my attentive supporters hover, I realize how much they care for me. They too want to keep my recovery intact. If people are truly wondering about that soda I am sipping on, it's their problem, not mine. Explaining my choice not to drink is something I don't need to spend my time worrying about. I can't be engulfed in mindless gossip, if there is any. Maintaining my sobriety is always the first priority, regardless of how I choose to resolve these sticky situations.

Questioning Mind

"Is it really necessary that I leer at my sister, who is simply having a glass of wine with dinner?" "Seriously, must I count how many beer bottles are in the recycling bin after my neighbor's party?" "Why do I care so much about my friends' new basement with that stellar wine cellar?" "Am I truly wondering, how in God's name that guy is only drinking a Coke at this party?"

"Why in the world am I focusing on the woman near me who just ordered her second cocktail in twenty minutes?" "What's wrong with those picnickers in the park; their table only has pitchers of lemonade on it?" "Do I sincerely need to pursue all the reasons why my brother-in-law doesn't allow alcohol on his boat?"

"Why am I concerned that my old friends choose not to drink alcohol when I am around?" "Am I thoroughly counting the amount of liquor on that shelf?" "Is it necessary that I stare at the servers' trays stacked with beer bottles?" "Am I really salivating over this tequila commercial when I never even liked the stuff?"

"Why is the clinking of ice cubes in a glass giving me the urge to have a real drink?" "Did that sign really say 'No alcohol permitted here'?" "Am I *really* staring with desire at that homeless man who is holding a brown paper bag to his mouth?" "Do I honestly have the right to say something to the gal next to me who is totally drunk?"

"Why am I always calculating how much everyone is drinking during the holidays?" "Why do I continue to glare at those who can partake in a cocktail?" "Why do I care about this kind of stuff?" "Why does my brain have to work like this all the time?" "Why?"

Because I am an alcoholic, that's why!

Purpose in This Life

I have a purpose in this life. I am meant to be on this earth. There are a million reasons why I should be here. I am supposed to be walking this course. I realize that I have a complicated past, but that must not grant me any excuse to quit moving forward.

I suffer with a curious disease not understood by many. Their misconception about alcoholism does not need to consume me. I know what I have to deal with, and I plan to do it. I have a goal, which keeps me motivated. I am fully aware of the consequences which may result from inaction. I have a true purpose today.

I am proud of who I have become. I have a place in the world where I am loved and needed. I'm aware of my strengths, and I know how to use them. I'm supposed to be here for the sake of others. I'm a tool in the toolbox, a piece of the puzzle, and a plant in the garden. I'm alive to fill my purpose.

I can do things. My talents are flowing free and touching others. I'm moving forward in discovering them. I'm gaining sensibilities and comprehending realities with a sound mind. I'm willing to seek out all that I was meant to be on this planet. The search for this kind of peace has been miraculous and rewarding. I arise with purpose.

I have monumental resolve to walk this course. I'm continuing to find buried treasure along the way. I can honestly count all the reasons I should be here. My heart is swelling with happiness and spirit. I have been given a second chance and a new lease on life. My complicated past has been set aside; I'm supposed to be here today because I have regained my human worth and purpose.

Our Disease Can Be Fatal

The disease of alcoholism can kill us. Because there is a stigma attached to our illness, many obituaries are written with a veiled single-mindedness meant to hide the real cause. Claiming that someone died this way would only result in unjust gossip and unwarranted ridicule. The truth is more easily measured when descriptions such as "accident," "kidney failure," "diabetes," or "liver disease" are used. The term *sudden death* is much easier to deal with than the word *suicide*.

Even today, as the awareness of addiction grows, the label of alcoholism still bears a shameful mark. So, the cover-up for our fatal malady is simply a safety valve, protecting our families and friends from the unpleasant chatter by those who consider problem drinking a moral weakness.

Strangely enough, when we are drinking, we accept all the possibilities of death. Oftentimes, we wish it upon ourselves. We easily dismiss our aching livers, continued falls, and physical deterioration. We come to believe that this kind of horrible end is our deserved fate and warranted punishment for our choices.

The disease of alcoholism can be fatal. It wasn't just a car accident. Her fall wasn't because the stairs were wet. He didn't just die in his apartment alone, at the age of thirty. She didn't suddenly go into cardiac arrest because of diabetes. His kidneys didn't stop working because he was on a healthy diet. Sclerosis of the liver wasn't diagnosed because she stuck with sparkling water. The cunning disease wouldn't let up, and the drinker simply couldn't break away from its powerful grip. This real-life destruction happens every day.

The mental and physical harm of our illness is sadly genuine. Today, I am choosing not to become one of its statistics. Today, I can be content in feeling healthy and strong. Today, I have the commitment to say no to its alluring lies which could lead me to death.

Possible Relapse

"I surely didn't think that would happen to him." "She couldn't have started drinking again; she had years of sobriety." "They both were always so helpful at meetings. This can't be possible." "My God, he was sponsoring three people." "She was always at every AA meeting." "They sure acted like they had it all together." "I would never have guessed that it would happen to him."

These were a few of my thoughts when I first learned that the potential for relapse was a reality. People I had emulated and looked up to with confidence had somehow succumbed to that moment when the perplexing temptation of alcohol strikes.

Of course, I knew that on any given day, the alcoholic could opt for the drink. I knew that the odds of it happening were great. I had read and reread all kinds of statistics. But to witness it in action, to see it take someone who you thought was no longer capable of falling, set me straight immediately. My disease was as cunning as a snake, always ready to pounce, always willing to lie.

Relapse was real. It wasn't just for some other person out there somewhere who wasn't working his recovery. It wasn't an anonymous individual who simply thought one drink at a party would be all right. I would hear people say, "Sue hasn't been around for a while, and I'm worried." Or, "Bob ended up back in rehab after two years." The nagging possibility was always lurking.

After witnessing one relapse after another, I suddenly realized that my disease was permanent; it wasn't cured, and it wasn't over. I came to understand that giving up the bottle wasn't just some passing fancy, meant to last for a few months. I understood that my recovery was a daily process, melding into the future. Maintaining sobriety was a lifelong commitment which could never be altered. Relapse was, in fact, very possible if I didn't stand firm in sobriety and commit to this new direction for life.

Making the Choice

I can't exactly pinpoint the moment when I finally acknowledged that I was an alcoholic. There were so many times when I should have conceded the truth. The mistakes and consequences over the years had racked up, but they never seemed to be enough to make me want to stop. I was willing to excuse and ignore all the obvious errors.

When I got my DUI, I felt totally ashamed for a few months and watched what I drank. I somehow managed to recover from the embarrassment by rushing straight back to the bottle. The blackouts bothered me for a day or so, but I usually forgot about them in a matter of time. When my family and friends began ignoring me, I told myself that it wasn't my fault. Preferring to be alone was something I wanted anyway.

As the tension between my spouse and I escalated with each passing day, I cast it off as typical relationship problems. The deterioration of my marriage certainly wasn't going to override my desire to drink. Even the morning shakes and vomiting didn't sound off the alarm that alcohol was the real problem. It was easier to avoid each and every one of these issues by drinking as soon as I could.

I was able to find an excuse for anything in order to

continue this way of life. As my relationships began to fail due to my intoxication, I couldn't be bothered to figure it out. If I got fired from work, then so be it; I could always find another job. By the end, I simply didn't care about who I hurt, or how many mistakes I made. Alcohol was the only thing I wanted and needed to survive.

Finally, my mental state and bodily decay unnerved me. I was completely exhausted from the drudgery of my daily life. I was weary of buying bottles, hiding bottles, and looking for them. I was depleted by the loneliness and the binding shame which gruesomely attacked me each day. I desperately missed my family and friends. I was embarrassed, frustrated, and empty. I was drained by the amount of time it took to cover up all my mistakes. I could no longer deal with the stress of my shattered existence. It was over. I just couldn't take it anymore. I was sick and tired of being sick and tired. With this came the only realistic conclusion: I needed help with my serious drinking problem.

Role Model in Life

My every intention in life was to be a role model for others. I was an intelligent youngster eager to reach the stars. I earnestly worked hard in school, and I strived to do my best. I made mistakes, and sometimes I made a mess of things, but I always tried to correct them. I fought life's struggles, like we all do. Usually, I was able to conquer setbacks.

I governed myself with sound principles. I was often proud of my resolute character. When I faced difficult times, I tried to learn from them. I knew how to make myself feel guilty when having opted for the wrong thing. I was the type who rooted for the underdog and usually accepted almost anyone. I was always serious about helping those who had less than I had. Charity played a huge part in my life. I took in the stray dogs and lost souls more than once. I had faith in God and faith in my own beliefs.

My every intention from the very beginning was to be a role model in life...until alcohol took it all away. There in the throngs of the bottle, I quickly lost every decent piece of myself. I became the polar opposite of everything I had set out to be. My once-principled character dissolved into a wasteland of lies and unconscious living, meant only for myself and my desires to remain drunk.

In recovery, I have rediscovered all those precious qualities I once held dear. I am now regaining all those profound sensibilities I once cherished. I am replacing the bottle with service and commitment toward a greater good in myself and others. I have opened my arms to sobriety where the opportunities to model wholesome living can be exemplified once more.

The Freedom of Confession

I made a lot of mistakes during my drinking days. I carried the heavy baggage, seemingly accrued from years of unconscious living. As my mind slowly started to clear, I began to realize how much harm I had caused to those I loved. I had truly hurt a lot of people.

I needed to make amends.

Before I could start to apologize for anything, I had to first concede to myself that I was powerless over alcohol, and that the unmanageability of my life had produced some serious destruction. There were some dark places I needed to face. Acknowledging these real issues opened the door to progressing toward the atonement of my past. I realized that the only way to resolve this was to own up to everything that I had done.

The term *confession* always sounded foreboding and slyly sinister. I viewed it as this dreary, joyless course which only left the sinner feeling some kind of gloomy remorse. I was truly frightened by all the ominous fabrications doled out in books and movies. I wasn't sure that I could actually take that step without being ridiculed by the person listening to my grievous admissions. I had a whole lot of bad behavior to discuss.

But with the beginnings of real sobriety under my belt, I managed to let go of all those misunderstood descriptions of what confession was truly meant to be. As I sat alongside my sponsor, I opened up my heart with a sincere honesty of the sordid details of my past. In this place of sanctity, another alcoholic listened to my aching admissions.

She did not finger-point, nor did she judge me. Instead, a quiet understanding filled our space. I began to sense a lightness of being, allowing my sorrows to stream forward without reservation. I was able to name my mistakes with a freedom I could hardly believe.

I was released from the burdens I had carried for so long. The result was not that of some morbid experience ending in years of bleak imprisonment. I was not sent away to be scourged for my errors. No, quite the opposite happened. I was given permission to forgive my own wrongdoing, which then enabled me to reach out and apologize to those I had harmed. Confession was a beautiful step toward the liberation of my soul and recovery.

I'm Not Going to Make It

"Right now, I just don't think that I'm going to make it." "Perhaps I should focus on breathing for an hour. Then I can take a little sip after that, should I so choose." "Sixty minutes is not that long." "Why am I thinking like this today?" "Maybe I ought to take a long, brisk walk; surely that might ease this uncontrollable urge." "God, I know I should be calling my sponsor, but I'd hate to admit how I'm feeling." "I'll give myself a little more time."

"I'm sick and tired of dealing with this stupid disease already." "I've really been dealt a terrible hand." "It's not fair that I have to go through this." "The liquor store is one mile away. Maybe I should drive by just to see what happens. Or I could walk in and say hello to the cashier; I'm sure he misses me." "Okay, stop that; you're not going anywhere."

"I really ought to call my sober friends. Maybe not; it wouldn't be polite to disrupt their day with my petty problems." "Well, there's always the wine aisle in the grocery store; I'm out of laundry detergent anyway." "Jeez, I'm really pushing the envelope." "Thirty minutes left, and then I'll go."

"I'd better find a meeting quick; I'm feeling pretty defenseless." "Nope, I'm going to manage this alone. I need to learn to be strong." "I've suffered through this whole recovery gig long enough; it's time I got off this wagon." "That's right, I've proved to everyone that I can behave." "I've paid my dues; it's time to move on."

"Hmmm, the very last time I drank, I made a fool of myself." "I don't know, I guess I did cause a lot of chaos, not to mention trouble for my family." "I certainly wasn't pleasant to anyone." "Those hangovers were pretty darn unbearable." "Ten more minutes and I get to decide." "I forgot about losing my job over too many sick days." "Maybe, just maybe, I wasn't that great of a drinker."

"All right, it's been an hour, and I'm still sober and alive." "Thank God I got through that; I think I'm going to try one more hour and get my sponsor on the line." "I'm amazed at how proud I am of myself." "I didn't pick up that drink, and I am doing just fine." "Right now, I think I'm going to make it and stick to recovery a little while longer."

What Time Is It?

"What time is it?" I need some water. "How did I land on this couch?" Maybe I'll make it a Coke instead. "Why am I still in my clothes?" I might want to make some toast. "Why does my face look blotchy?" Maybe I ought to sit down. "Where did I put my cigarettes?" I need to think for a second. "Who did I call last night?" Coffee might rejuvenate my brain. "Did I stay up that late?" Surely a hot shower should help. "How could I be this exhausted?" I've run out of clean towels. "Is my husband mad at me again?" I'd better do some laundry this afternoon.

"Okay, what did I do last night?" Let me walk around the house for a minute. "Did I really leave the lunch meat out?" It couldn't have been me. "Now, what time is it?" I may want to relax for a bit. "Why is my head pounding?" Aspirin should do the trick. "Who knocked over the picture frame?" That darn dog. "Where's my lighter?" Smoking a cigarette might juggle my memory. "How did the ashtray get broken?" There's way too much crap in this house anyway.

"Can I manage a few chores this afternoon?" I need to finish this coffee first. "Did I offend somebody? I got the feeling I did." My mind never seems to work right on Mondays. "Who was yelling at me last night?" I must have had a nightmare.

"Should I be concerned about something?" I think I have the flu. "What happened yesterday?" Another cigarette will help. "Why in the world am I letting these crazy thoughts bother me?" I'll figure these problems out later. "Now where in the world did I put my booze?"

For Those Who Had No Choice

Alcoholism affects everyone around us. We don't see it then, nor do we deliberately set out to cause others harm. Usually, when we are captivated by our drunken stupors, we don't even recognize that actual chaos is ensuing. Sometimes we might hurt people physically. Most times, we slowly destroy our relationships with an unwavering resolve to remain intoxicated. Our loved ones are emotionally bruised by our inability to distinguish how badly we are wounding them.

One afternoon while I was in rehab, a counselor, while praying, said this: "for those children who never had the choice." My immediate reaction was to pity those kids suffering in dilapidated homes as their parents drank the hours away. I concluded that this sort of prayer applied to someone else, somewhere else. It couldn't possibly pertain to any of the chaos I had caused. What I had done was surely different.

But in mere moments, the wall came tumbling down as I suddenly realized that my drinking had affected my own children. I was nowhere near perfect when I was intoxicated. Most of the time, I wasn't even present. I instantly understood that I had caused them endless pain. I was responsible for this. The insurmountable turmoil had occurred under my own roof, not someone else's. If I wanted to do any finger-pointing, it should be at myself.

This was a crashing reality as I maneuvered my way through recovery. This piercing awareness allowed me to accept the harrowing injuries of my disease. I had hurt my children. I had pushed them aside. I had not always met their needs. My children had not been given the choice, and the time had come for me to admit this.

Simple Pleasures
of Sobriety

For years, I didn't feel anything. For years, I didn't do anything. For years, I attached myself to the bottle, while desperately clinging to the perpetual need for isolation. My mere existence had become that undeniably simplified.

I didn't participate in any aspect of life. I loathed parties, events, and gatherings of any kind. My spirit was only stirred by booze. Fun was unfathomable. Laughter, long gone. I barely contributed to the world around me. I did not join in, nor did I share any meaningful part of myself with anyone. I was merely a silent observer, watching how other people lived. I ignored my deep desire to join them. Alcohol helped me erase that urging. It spurned me on to that crucial drunken stupor where I could forget these festering concerns.

When I finally chose recovery, I was a bit surprised by the simple pleasures of a normal day. It was as if I were learning to relive again. The most basic satisfactions of an ordinary routine had long been forgotten. In almost a childlike manner, I was suddenly discovering the tiniest comforts in the world around me.

Laughter is an amazing sound. Clean sheets feel refreshing.

Blankets are soft. Exercise is invigorating. Work completes a day. Friendships are meant for sharing. Animals are nice to pet. Family is nice to have around. The sun actually shines, and the rain is indeed wet.

Food tastes good. Hot showers begin a day. Parties are usually enjoyable. Clean clothes smell crisp. A stranger's smile is uplifting. Learning something new is interesting. Movies really do have endings. Conversations are fulfilling. Flowers do emit fragrant aromas. Soda tastes sweet and bubbly. A lit candle softens a room. The sunset is beautiful. The joy of loving another is genuinely pure.

One single day, one day at a time, free from the bondage of the bottle, can be filled with unique blessings and great awakenings. All those wasted years of feeling nothing are now in the past. I have learned to embrace the simplest pleasures of daily living.

Alcoholic Anxiety

I could not understand why I couldn't stop drinking. I tried to quit with every ounce of energy I could possibly muster. Everyone around me could easily have a few cocktails, and then finish the night with a cup of coffee. I simply couldn't fathom how they knew right when to quit. I was very troubled by my unnatural lack of ability to stop when they did.

My developing confusion eventually changed to intensifying fear. How could I tell anyone that I really needed alcohol? How could I explain that drinking had become my daily obsession? How could I admit to this kind of weakness? Stating my concerns would only lead to finger-pointing and ridicule. I felt terribly alone in the world.

Sure, the term *alcoholic* was not new to me. Members of my own family had been given that label. I knew a lot of people who gossiped about those "problem drinkers." I knew that I fit in that category, but I also knew that I didn't want to be branded that way. Worse, I couldn't imagine having an enjoyable lifestyle absent of alcohol. A confession of this kind would truly imprison me in the teetotaler's world. These sort of concerns were always on my mind.

I harbored these thoughts as the intensity of my anxiety

continued to grow. I spent most nights fitfully turning in my bed, as forlorn images of my future pounded my brain. Unfortunately, these dire apprehensions only forced me to drink more. It was the only way to maintain any sense of peace.

Finally, I could no longer tolerate this daily, impending dread. I was physically and emotionally beaten. My misgivings about what other people thought of me no longer seemed to matter. If I had to be chastised, so be it. I honestly didn't care anymore; I was desperately ill, and I knew it. My life was in shambles. I was clearly not a normal drinker; I had a definite problem with alcohol. I could no longer face this wretched disease on my own. I was ready and wholeheartedly willing to take a step forward to save myself.

Alcoholics Are Not Weak

Those who don't understand addiction usually classify alcoholics as weak-minded types, just the kind of persons who lack character and a moral compass. I believed that myself for quite some time. Back then when the bottle ran my life, I just couldn't understand how I could not stop the daily desire to have it. How had I become so feeble in my thinking? Where was that courageous person who could eagerly challenge herself? What happened to the free thinking, convincing, resilient human being who knew how to take on the tough times? At what point did I allow alcohol to reign over all the most important things in my life?

Addiction comes in all shapes and sizes. It is sly and progressive. It chooses us with a madness of contempt and erosion. It condemns our very soul to an absolute need of only what it wants from us. It takes us to despondent places where our choices are dissolved into bleak, habitual desires which cannot be tamed. We eventually accept our insanity in some kind of meaningless agreement. The very concept of normal living is gone.

Addiction is a disease. Just like any other disease, there is a form of treatment which we must adhere to in order to become strong and vibrant again. There is no medication or man-made drug which can formally heal our desire to drink. The sickness will always be with us. But that monstrous little voice urging us to drink can be destroyed by our willingness to work in recovery. It is absolutely possible to gather the courage to change our behavior. We can choose to be powerful in this decision by participating in the AA fellowship, employing a sponsor, praying to our Higher Power, working the twelve steps, and helping other alcoholics. These are the imperative tools which help us maneuver through the challenges of maintaining a sober life.

We are not weak because we choose to be strong. We arise with commitment to face our battles, and we intend to win. We are brave because we are willing to adhere to a plan. We push ourselves forward, ultimately deciding that we *can* change our lives just one day at a time.

From Darkness to Light

We will come out of the darkness and see a great light. We will rise from the depths of despair. We will come to know an incredible freedom, the one we have been searching for all this time. We will realize our gifts and finally put them to use. We will feel this momentum and no longer seek the fruitless promises of intoxication.

We will find fulfillment in helping others. We will choose victory over sorrow. We will learn how to stride in accomplishment. We will face all things with honesty and hope. We will change our path in a contented direction. We will march forward with nerves of steel.

We will create peace within our souls. We will cherish every moment of this renewed choice. We will grow with each passing day. We will sense the comfort of meaningful determination. We will make choices with the pulse of a sound mind. We will be satisfied with the abundant results.

We will witness a transformation which we never thought possible. We will suddenly recognize grace. We will feel the strength surge as we follow this course. We will be awed by this incredible shift from what we were like before. We will be granted this miracle of everlasting serenity when we finally step forward into the light of sobriety.

The Bottle Was My Voice

Eventually the bottle spoke for me. Its boiling liquid pulsated throughout my body with wild contempt. Alcohol slowly overtook even the tiniest piece of goodness which I had once counted on as a human being. Each day I grew more inflamed as it continued to generate heightened anger and pounding fear.

My outbursts raged on with every sip. I became lost in a despondent form of nagging hatred. I could not find optimism in any part of my day. I grew to believe that nobody could do what I wanted, and I began to loath their presence with utter disdain. I found reasons to ridicule everything around me. I couldn't wait to destroy any happy event. Mocking decent people who were fulfilling their lives became one of my favorite pastimes. I detested anyone who made sense.

My personality became brash, rude, and often startling. I was always satisfied when I conquered the next creature who dared minimize my opinion. I gravitated toward the fight and was willing to attack. Intoxication caused me to inflict emotional pain with no real remorse. Listening to any viewpoint other than my own was entirely out of the question.

I prided myself in being antagonistic. My wrath could be

justly poured out on a mere stranger at the bar. Irritation escalated with every bottle of booze I swallowed. Whatever the situation, there was always something wrong with it. My resentments sprouted with each passing drink, granting me permission to behave unkindly.

Alcohol spoke loud and clear, pouring out insult after insult. It devoured any reasonable sensibility I once claimed. I was spellbound by its ferocious calamity. I was entirely absorbed by the madness and utter erosion of my soul. And I couldn't help it; I couldn't stop it. I had ultimately given it my voice.

Please Return to Us

"Please come back to us." I heard that phrase from everyone who loved me. At first, I didn't quite understand what they meant; I was standing right there. Every once in a while, my friends bashfully hinted that I was drinking a bit too much. I chalked it off as a happy-hour routine. My siblings chided me about my depreciating physical appearance. The image I perceived in the mirror looked perfectly normal to me.

My children chastised me about my lack of routine. I rebuked their nagging by telling myself that teenagers were normally disrespectful. Some of my distant relatives expressed perplexity when listening to my muffled voice messages. I excused that questioning by claiming that I needed a newer phone. My spouse constantly badgered me about my insolent behavior. I promptly ignored this by seeking refuge in another room.

Everyone I knew was slyly trying to persuade me to join them in the land of the living. They cautiously pointed out my concerning drinking habits. I knew that their comments were only meant to help me. By then, I was already committed to the ghostly calling of the bottle and the desire to achieve further invisibility.

While driven by the need to hide from those who loved me, I quietly contemplated their unease regarding my countenance. But in order to remain safe from that pain, I actively created a phantom life whereby their words could no longer be felt.

I distinctly knew what was meant when they asked me to return. I noticed myself changing long before my friends said a word. I could feel the disease wrecking my body prior to my siblings' observations. I knew that my conversational voice was slurred and tainted most of the time. I recognized that my spouse had reasons to hassle me eons before he actually did. And I absolutely understood that I was plagued with the desire to drink way before I actually prioritized this obsession over the requests of my children.

But I could not stop drinking for the sake of anyone, least myself. By then, I had learned to shelve away every offer persuading me to return to normal living. I had made a commitment to dissolve all that was left of me into a bottle. And so I lived alone, with loved ones right beside me, choosing to ignore their pleading requests.

One Is Too Many

One is too many, and a thousand isn't enough. One drink will lead to another, and then another after that. A little tilt of that alcoholic beverage causes an awakening within us. We will irrationally want more. The outright need turns into obsession, which cannot be stopped.

This insane craving is perplexing to all normal drinkers, who seem to know when to quit. They can't comprehend this phenomenon which causes our brains to ask for more booze, regardless of the time or day. Once we are in the grips of it, ceasing is never an option.

When we ponder the years of our alcoholic experience, we can easily see that our drive to drink was actually spurned on by our first gulp of booze. The initial sip was always the culprit. Although our alcoholic patterns may have varied, our outcomes were generally the same. Some of us drank at home, while others frequented the bars. Many of us drank daily while others binged heavily on weekends. Some of us preferred liquor, while others opted for beer.

Some of us could drink all day, while others carried on into the night.

It didn't matter how we did it or what flavor we chose;

the final result always managed to prove that we just couldn't stop. Being connoisseurs of the alcoholic sort usually meant consequences, which inevitably occurred because we drank that first one.

The only sure remedy for this is to painstakingly avoid it. There is no other option; our course of action has to start there. One tilt of the glass for any of us will lead to an obsession which will irrationally permeate our every move. It will not cease in its battle to take us over.

We know that a tiny drop can perpetrate problems quicker than we realize. Because for us, one is too many, and a thousand isn't enough.

Rewinding the Tape

Once in a while, my mind tempts me into wanting that drink. Sometimes it's the smallest things which can set me off; other times, it's those booming celebrations which cause me to waver. And if I am to be perfectly honest, there are those baffling moments when that alcoholic thinking whispers to me for no reason at all.

I've heard that devilish voice before, slyly prompting me to make that poor decision which leads to an inevitable consequence. I must squash it immediately. In order to regain my senses, I quickly pray. This gives me breathing room and a moment of direction where I can maximize all of my options. I can call my sponsor, run to an AA meeting, or dial another alcoholic. I am not in this alone; I have tools to get me through it.

Another route which always sets me straight is to replay the old tape of myself when I was running with the bottle. One quick glance is really enough to wake me up. I turn back the clock, remembering how pathetic I was when I was wasted. I just call up the "old me," slurring her words, lying about everything, blacking out, not making sense, isolating from everyone, hiding bottles, forgetting where she put them, embarrassing family and friends, falling down, causing chaos, ruining parties, getting sick, shaking, forgetting important dates, passing out, disappearing into darkness, covering up her shame, slipping into unconscious living, grasping for silence, hating the world, fighting everyone, and hoping the end will come soon.

That's right; a slight glimpse of my past shows me exactly why I can never pick up a drink again. That immediate review highlights every single reason why I can't go back there. Rewinding my tape has become a wake-up call for the present whenever I sense that vulnerable moment of possible relapse.

Why?

"Why am I thinking about drinking tonight? It's only Tuesday, for God's sake." "Why am I obsessed with the fact that the boss is throwing a party without alcohol? It shouldn't be the end of the world." "Why am I angry that we have to leave the party so early? You'd think that by midnight I would have had enough." "Why am I worried about how much liquor is in the house? Most people aren't contemplating this in the middle of the afternoon."

"Why am I buying more wine for the cellar? Anybody could look down there and see that we have enough for a year." "Why am I stopping at the bar for just one before I go home? My friends tend to go to the grocery store instead." "Why am I deliberating whether I'm going to partake in an adult beverage at dinner? Everyone else is discussing what they're going to be cooking."

"Why am I using the excuse that alcohol helps me sleep? Most people choose other options, like warm milk." "Why am I concerned that I keep waking up on the couch? I really thought that I made it upstairs last night." "Why am I hiding that bottle of liquor in the laundry room closet? Everyone I know uses the kitchen cupboard or built-in bar." "Why am I making up stories when I see the cashier at the liquor store? Most people just walk in and purchase their stuff without lying."

"Why am I totally obsessing about how much I'm drinking? Everybody else seems to know when to quit." "Why am I excusing my bad behavior last night? My other friends never cause that sort of commotion at bars." "Why am I unable to go for a day without having one? Most people can go without it for weeks." "Why am I even talking to myself like this? I'm beginning to wonder why I keep having to ask myself these questions."

Desire to Help another Alcoholic

The desire to help another alcoholic was automatic. After I came to terms with my drinking problem and accepted the truth of my condition, I wanted to scream from the mountaintops with an echoing hope. Yes, I suffered from a perplexing disease, but it could be managed by a Higher Power if you were only willing to let go. I longed to get on a loudspeaker to announce that sobriety was attainable and a wonderful way to live.

I couldn't wait to explain that through hard work and dedication, serenity could actually be achieved. I wanted to touch that individual still drinking to let them know that life was possible without it. I was filled with an exuberant message that sobriety was an amazing gift.

I ached to convey that I definitely struggled sometimes but found the means to get through it. I deeply wanted all those still lingering in the shadows to step forward so that I could share the joys of change and forgiveness. The immense force toward helping the next person encompassed me. My newly discovered way of life was the prize of all prizes.

I could barely contain my own personal story of grace,

and I fought hard for those still straddling the fence. I empathized with their pain by acknowledging my own. My words were filled with hope and compassion. I deeply wanted them to know that recovery actually worked.

The desire to help another alcoholic was an automatic reaction. Normal living, without the insanity of alcohol, was an incredible journey of true freedom. I had finally come to understand this. I couldn't wait to share my experience, strength, and hope with that person who was still suffering.

Alcohol Is a Cunning Snake

Alcohol is a cunning snake, wrapping around us with suffocating intensity. It knows exactly when to strike. It waits for just the right moment when our emotions are floundering and our strength is wavering. It hears our misguided thoughts and our dramatic lamentations. It uses our weaknesses to trap us. It compels us to drain our worries into unconscious safety.

Alcohol is a powerful snake, gnashing at our innermost fears with bloodied bites. It sits quietly in the corner anticipating our need to awaken past hurts. It adores our over exaggerated feelings. It attacks our natural desire to maintain normalcy in our thinking. It can't wait to pounce on our most fragile moments.

Alcohol is a baffling snake, appearing with the disguise of friendship, rushing toward us with promises of kindness. It knows how deeply penetrated we are when we are placed in vulnerable situations. It is quick to soften the blow and purposely present when we look for courage. It convinces us that we can tackle our deepest weaknesses.

Alcohol is a sly snake, silently moving toward us with a tempered resolve. It understands that we need to be comforted. Its nip cures us of our feelings of inadequacy and smallness.

It senses our wavering uncertainties. It swirls into our hearts with the makings of a peaceful beat. It eases our reactions and simplifies our worries.

Alcohol is a fateful snake, luring us toward unnoticed bodily harm. It is discreet in its minimized realities of our intake. It softly removes any of these concerns. It preys on our numbed mind. It gently places bandages over our wounds. It sneakily promotes forgetting. It becomes our only ally. Its victory is the moment we become fully bound to it. Once this diabolical accomplishment is in place, it sits back snickering, as our very souls slowly begin to die.

Courage

Our disease created a weakened mind. It numbed our thoughts, which inevitably failed us each time we tried to quit drinking. This confusion created the illusion that we were morally defunct, helplessly unprincipled, and completely ineffective in our will to fix this problem.

But that was how it looked on the outside. Deep down, we longed to mend this exhausting way of living. And we toyed with ourselves daily, wondering how it would feel if we actually admitted that alcohol was destroying our lives. We knew; we were just mustering up the strength to own up to this fact. Surrender, change, and acceptance took a great deal of courage.

Eventually, the grueling warfare of our soul relented to defeat. We had grown weary of the battle and somehow decided that we could risk it all, daring to be brave. We had become powerless over alcohol; we could no longer control it alone.

This is insurmountable courage, my friend. This is the kind of uncertain honesty which many out there will never disclose. Conceding to ourselves and others that we need help is a bold beginning. It takes nerves of steel to finally say it aloud.

No, we were never weak-minded; we were merely

subsisting on the lies of the bottle. We knew within our innermost self that our cunning disease was controlling our lives. Perhaps we were only patiently waiting to assemble the necessary step to finally take this first step—the most courageous decision we would ever make.

Sitting in Serenity

I am sitting in serenity, a place where I have found peace. I have acclimated to recovery and have accepted my alcoholism. I am quiet now, one with the tranquility of normal living. I am breathing in the stillness of faith and joy. I am relaxed in the presence of only today.

I am whole again. I am comforted by my surroundings. I am free of fear, resentment, and anxious thinking. I am walking in the light. I no longer have the desire to drink. I am fully contented by this. I am committed to sobriety with an amazing energy and strength. I am sitting in serenity, a place where I have found peace. I have made my way out of the darkness; I have found a new place where healing shines upon me.

I am okay in the here and now. I am solid and composed, no longer tormented by what used to be. I am incredibly still. I am sitting in serenity where I have finally come to know the true meaning of leading a healthy life, surrounded by comfort, harmony, and love.

Funeral for Myself

I attended my own funeral, somewhere in the beginning of sobriety. Of course, this was not an actual, physical death. This was the deliberate decision to put that raging alcoholic to rest. I wanted to rejoice in this passing, for it was necessary and good. I wanted to celebrate it with strength, willingness, and fortitude; those same virtues I began using when I made the choice to recover.

And yet, when it came to be, when I accepted that it should be, I lingered there for one last momentary glimpse of the woman who was. I wanted to hold her lifeless hand. I wanted to kiss her face and close my eyes to the memory of her. I wanted to take her into my arms one last time in compassion and forgiveness. I needed to tell her that she would not be forgotten, for she would always be a part of me, stored away in the secret compartment of my heavy heart.

This was my wake, the remembrance of a life which had not been well-lived under the powerful force of the bottle. My silent reverence ached with all the recollection of that very sick person who had been eaten away by fear and hopelessness. These loitering thoughts shifted between profound heartache and grateful release.

I needed to bury that shattered, frail human being who had desperately wavered between restless hours of reality and prevailing stretches of despondent intoxication. It was time for her to sleep in a comfortable place, where her tireless longing for peace would finally be realized.

I gazed one last time with a solemn glance, whispering a final good-bye. I stepped away knowing that I could never look back, for she would be gone, settled in the crevices of yesterday.

I wiped the tears from my face, sighing in contented release, and turned toward my sober future where the beginnings of rebirth and new life awaited me.

The Screaming
Has Stopped

The screaming has stopped now. The nightmares have lessened. The untamed habits have diminished. The scourge has healed. The nameless days have dissolved. The relationships have mended. The apologies have been accepted. The restlessness has eased. The wild emotions have decreased. The angered tirades have been minimized.

The pain has softened. The outrageous tempers have been reduced. The sorrowful panic has become restrained. The thoughtless thinking has been streamlined. The quaking of old memories has refrained. The useless causes have been cut back. The self-loathing has fled. The past patterns have been worked on. The list of weaknesses has shortened. The list of strengths has grown.

The sleepless nights have been comforted. The agonizing mistakes, slowly resolved. The confessions have been spoken. The truths have been confronted. The nagging desires have been subdued. The persistent fears have been exposed. The prodding anxieties have unraveled. The poetic lies have been erased. The fruitless promises have been buried. The hidden burdens have been unearthed.

The screaming has stopped now. The haunting dreams have decreased. The good changes have multiplied. The friendships have expanded. The pursuit for freedom has opened. The bravery has intensified. The resolve has amplified. The normalcy has been created. The thankfulness has been pronounced. The heart has been enlarged. The surrender has been fulfilled. The suffering has ended. The new life has been lovingly altered. The pursuit for sobriety has been embraced now, one day at a time.

Lightning Source UK Ltd.
Milton Keynes UK
UKHW021331220321
380778UK00012B/2879